Common Sense Entrepreneurial Management

Building a Better Business in Spite of Yourself

By

Paul E. Balus

authorHOUSE™

1663 LIBERTY DRIVE, SUITE 200
BLOOMINGTON, INDIANA 47403
(800) 839-8640
WWW.AUTHORHOUSE.COM

First published by AuthorHouse 11/01/04

ISBN: 1-4184-0542-6 (sc)

Library of Congress Control Number: 2004105068

Printed in the United States of America
Bloomington, Indiana

This book is printed on acid-free paper.

Table of Contents

Acknowledgments

I would like to "thank" all the owners and managers I have had the pleasure to work for and with throughout my career, both the good ones and the not-so-good ones. Regardless of their desire, motives, knowledge, and abilities, I have learned a great deal from each one of them.

I would especially like to "thank" my family: Kathy, Lindsey, Christopher, and Steve for their love, support, and encouragement.

And most important of all, I would like to "thank" my Lord Jesus Christ for the Love, Grace, and Mercy He gives to me each and every day.

About the Author

Paul Balus is the president and owner of CS Business Consultants and Marketing Solutions, Inc. He has held vice president positions in sales and business development with several marketing and promotional companies. In addition, he has held management positions with such companies as Colgate-Palmolive and American Home Products.

He has a Bachelor of Science degree in business administration from Southwest University in Louisiana. He currently holds a first and second degree black belt in karate, enjoys all types of outdoor activities, and loves to read and write. He also enjoys spending time helping serve others in and through his local church.

Paul and his wife Kathy have two children, a son-in-law, and a Scottish terrier named Zoe. Daughter Lindsey, son Christopher, son-in-law Steve, and Zoe all reside in the greater Minneapolis-St. Paul area.

Introduction

I have had the pleasure of working for some of the finest public companies in the United States. During my many years of employment with these firms, I have been given many opportunities to advance, not only in my business career, but also as a human being.

Starting my career as a sales representative covering two Midwestern states, I learned a lot about the entrepreneurial businessperson, what makes them tick, what makes them want to be their "own boss." It wasn't until I started to actually work for a private entrepreneurial businessperson that *I realized what a "real Entrepreneur" was!*

I'll delve into this unique character in the very first chapter of this book, so you won't have to wait long. I never really thought about writing a book before, certainly not one on this subject. I thought I would write about some mystery that took place hundreds of years ago or something fictional, maybe even a children's book. Come to think of it, this book you're about to read may very well cover all of the above.

The entrepreneur is somewhat of a mystery. Sometimes they seem so far removed from reality that they do indeed seem like a fictitious person, and many times they do act more like children than adults! That's probably a little harsh, but with all due respect, the only reason I chose this topic to write about is because there is such a great need out there for a plain, common sense book to help this untamed, unorganized, self-anointed King of the Business World that I find myself writing this.

Yes, there are many business books out there written by PhDs or psychologists and so forth, but not many are structured with a common sense approach, geared towards the uncomplicated. As most people in business tend to reach for these "formulated books" that try to make business more complex, they get further away from the business basics that make a person and company very successful. I am not saying these books are bad; in fact, many are very good. It's just that the businessperson reading these books has forgotten or has never been exposed to the common sense basic business practices we all need to possess in order to become successful. This book is not just limited to the entrepreneur, but should be viewed as an opportunity for everyone who is in management to improve and grow, not only their own career, but also that of their employees and company.

A word of caution here: If you are an entrepreneur and your own boss and are unwilling to check your ego at the door, then don't read this book any further. In fact, put it down right now and run out of the store; run far and run fast! Why? Because this book is going to challenge how you think, how you treat your employees, and how you treat your own business.

If you have the courage to read about who you are or who you have become and what you need to do to become the manager and possess the business you read about in the national business journals, then sit down, pour yourself something to drink, and enjoy this insight. As you read through this book, it is important to note that whatever you take away from this, even if it is only one point, it will make you a better person, manager, and entrepreneur.

Enjoy the read!

Chapter 1: In the Beginning, God Created the Entrepreneur

With everything our Lord created in the universe, the one creature that seems to continue to be a mystery—outside of Nessie and Bigfoot—is the entrepreneur. You know, the person who wants to be his or her own boss, direct his or her own company, and play by his or her own rules. The same person who wants to be in charge, play the part, yet refuses to do the right things to grow his or her business or the people who work there.

I do not think it is fair of me to paint the picture that everyone who has decided to go into business on their own is a bad manager or an untrained businessperson. On the contrary, I know there are many sharp, well-trained businesspeople operating their own businesses out there right now. I just haven't had the privilege of working for any.

I have worked for people who were fortunate in business deals or partnerships that allowed them the financial gain to finally "go it alone." I have worked for people who, through marriage or inheritance, have been put into positions to own and run their own businesses. I have also worked for people who had worked for major Fortune 500 companies, but forgot what they had been taught while working for such companies. In my opinion, this last one is the worst creature of all because they have had the most training, both in terms of general business and interpersonal management skills. Yet they have totally discarded the positive tools given to them to make them successful.

Ah yes, the entrepreneurs. God created these beings to literally drive the employees who work for them crazy. *The entrepreneur is a complicated person who seems to thrive on their own stress or the ability to create stress for those who work for them or with them.*

What makes these people tick? Who are they? Where do you find such a person? Well, the primary catalyst in the general makeup of the entrepreneur is the…yep, here it comes…the ego. The ego, the thing that yells out, "Hey, it's all about me, it's what I want, what I need and what I think." It's the same voice that says, "Don't tell me what needs to be done, what I should or shouldn't do. Remember, everyone wants to be me!"

Who are they? They may very well be you, or someone you work for or work with. They are not gender specific, although I can tell you that my historical data is taken from an all-male ensemble. Finding the entrepreneur is very easy because they are everywhere. They can be found in any private business, regardless of industry or trade.

Oh yes, one more thing that will identify an entrepreneur. This thing is one of the main reasons they get themselves and their companies in trouble. It is simply this. Entrepreneurs have no one above them to correct them, watch over them, slap them on the hands when they do stupid things. It is this same freedom that can propel them to success just as easily as it can make them become a failure.

Inasmuch as the entrepreneur can be difficult to deal with because of his or her inherent nature, it should be clearly noted that the entrepreneur is a person of great courage, adventure, and drive. I, like most people, should and do admire them for putting their necks on the line, for not only walking to the edge of the cliff, but also taking that leap of faith off of it. Too often, we are reluctant to move too far away from the security of our own shores and test the waters leading to distant lands and the riches and rewards that accompany such bravery.

Chapter 2: Managing Yourself–It Starts & Ends with Management

One of the hardest things to do as a person is to manage oneself. Manage your finances, manage your career path, manage your time and so on. The entrepreneur character and spirit compounds this difficulty. By nature, entrepreneurs usually do not have anyone above them, so they do not directly report to anyone, unless you include the bank or private investors, or possibly a very interested spouse!

Yes, in many cases, there is the bank or investors to report to because they do require some plan or idea as to how and when their return on investment will be realized. However, in the trenches, in the day-to-day activity of running the business or the investment, it is the entrepreneur who has complete authority. This is where entrepreneurs need to learn how to manage themselves.

With no one overseeing them, entrepreneurs walk a very tight rope between success and failure. They forget that every eye and every ear is watching and listening to every move they make and everything they say. Their employees may not speak up or seek changes by going through the proper channels (if in fact, there are procedures in place to air concerns); however, they will observe and start to formulate an opinion of management and the company they work for. As the owner/manager, you must ask yourself, what kind of opinion do you want your employees to have of you and your company? After all, they are or should be your biggest advocates in private, but more importantly, out in the public where you must value and guard your reputation.

It all starts and ends with management. There is no escaping this fact. You can run from it, pray it isn't true, and even put some kind of voodoo curse on it, but it will not change the simple fact that everything starts with you, the entrepreneur, the owner—you know "The Big Kahuna."

I have had owners who have berated me in front of customers (and no, this is not why I am writing this book), owners who have made razor-sharp comments and have been condescending to me in front of fellow employees, and owners who literally walked away from me when discussing business. The latter wasn't because they disagreed with my comments, it was because they had no interest in my opinions, and I was in charge of business development! The key to managing yourself is to evaluate your day-to-day activities and tasks. Ask yourself, if I was managing me right now, how would I direct myself? What would I recommend I do to ensure my success?

I'm sure almost everyone has heard of the saying *"you lead by example."* This is a very old saying; it probably started with the first caveman, but regardless of its origin, it is without doubt the single best leadership statement ever conceived. You do lead by example. The question is, what kind of example are you leading by?

I have worked for owners who possess what the psychologists call "passive-aggressive behavior." These are entrepreneurs who are also known as Dr. Jekyll and Mr. Hyde. They can be as kind and thoughtful as one could hope for, luring the unsuspecting employee into feeling all is right with the world, then in less than a New York second, turn into one of the meanest and cruelest creatures known to man. I have yet to see this person be able to capture the hearts and loyalty of his or her employees. In fact, *the owners and managers who possess this type of behavior usually are the root cause of their own business failure, regardless of the long-term potential success of their business.*

The entrepreneur who possesses this passive-aggressive behavior normally is not aware that he does have this problem. If you think you may have this and are asking yourself, why wouldn't someone tell me about my behavior? …Well, the mere fact that no one has should tell you something about yourself, shouldn't it?

I once worked with a person who was so absolutely terrified of the owner that she directly reported to, she couldn't even approach him on the simplest of things, such as clarifying a correct mailing address or asking him a question on a client order! This person came to me to ask a question only the owner could answer because she was so scared. If you have your own employees—especially the ones who are your right-hand associates—so totally scared, nervous, and confused, what are your realistic chances of having a successful business?

Ask yourself, how would I want to be managed and treated? How would you perform your tasks if you had to walk on eggs around your boss? One of the cardinal sins of management in any aspect of the business is setting your people up to fail. The failure can be as small as sending a piece of mail to the wrong address or can be as large as losing the top customer in your business. Highly successful entrepreneurs know that the first thing they must do is set the example for their team. They also have a very good understanding that they are, and will be, only as good as their employees allow them to be. Unless you are planning to be a single, one-person business, you need a very good, highly-qualified team of employees who will run through a wall for you. You want a team of open, honest, and loyal people who share the same desires and goals you have for your business.

What does this team of loyalists want from their company's owner? They want to be treated in the same positive manner you expect them to treat you and the business you started. Remember, it all starts and ends with management, and you are the management!

Chapter 3: Some People Fish, Some Golf, Some Have a Business!

As I previously mentioned, there are entrepreneurs who have achieved their monetary success through an inheritance, marriage, or a successful one-time business deal. The relationship between you and your business is very fragile at best under these circumstances. Sounds funny, doesn't it?

When you have been blessed with a situation where you have monetary success and feel like you want to start a business, think it through before you start the process. I am not saying don't, in fact, if you practice sound business management and people skills, it would be a great idea.

You would contribute jobs and money into the economy, and that is always a win-win proposition.

Regardless of your wealth or the availability of investment funds you have before you start your business, you would be well-advised to be reminded that you are starting a real business—a business that will more than likely employ a group of people who are counting on you to lead them to job security, career advancement, and financial prosperity. You should take this seriously, because the employees you hire will. They are counting on you to do everything possible to make the business and them successful. They have themselves and their families to take care of.

I know of entrepreneurs who—because of their wealth—either before or after they started their business, have allowed their businesses to become nothing more than a "hobby" for them. Their business has become a place to go to spend some time away from home, a place to see their name on an office building and a place to go to get their ego stroked. Unfortunately, it also becomes a place to go to "juice up the troops" as I like to call it. *"Juice up the troops" simply means to blow into the office, get everyone worked up into a frenzy, create a stir, then cut out, leaving an organizational stress level equal to a 10 megaton atomic bomb!*

People who, as they say, have "deep pockets" and get into business for the wrong reasons have a tendency to make very serious mistakes in how they manage, who they select to manage their businesses, and the overall choices they make concerning the long-term growth of that business. I have worked for business owners who expected their management staff to make sure their every need was being met. In fact, almost every second of the day, the president of the company and his staff were totally devoted to managing the expectations of the owner. News flash: if you own a business where your team is constantly managing your expectations, wants, and desires, telling you what they think you want to hear, then guess what— they are not managing the business where it counts…your customers and employees. *When you are constantly managing upward, you can't manage downward.*

In this situation, the president of the company and his staff were so busy managing the owner that they were simply not making the correct decisions to move the business to a successful level, or not making decisions at all.

The bottom line is this: If you have been blessed with the financial ability to go into business for yourself, put your name on a building front, and hire a group of people who need work, then take it seriously. If you are not going to take it seriously, then go fishing or take up golf. This way, the only one who will go crazy or get frustrated is you.

Chapter 4: They'll Let Any Tom, Dick, or Harry...

Once you have checked the ego at the door, realized that it all starts and ends with management, and that you need to take your business seriously, you can look at the staff you will need to hire.

One thing that has always bothered me about the hiring practice of employees by owners and managers is that they evaluate and hire in the short term and with very limited forward thinking. Owners are willing to hire people who are not qualified for the position they have available, just so they can fill a short-term immediate need the business has. In some cases, a business may hire someone who is overly qualified for this short-term need.

Paul E. Balus

Either direction will be bad for the business, especially for the employee and your customers.

A common management error when it comes to building your employee team is not fully grasping what assets your employee brings to the company. This error is not solely directed at the new or established entrepreneur, but is also directed at the private and public businesses that have more than a couple dozen employees. The well-managed companies train their managers to know their employees' business backgrounds inside and out, so they can maximize the employees' talents and contributions toward the overall success of the company.

Entrepreneur-owners must know the background of every employee if they are to put themselves in a position to take full advantage of the talents in which they have invested. As your business gets more successful and mature, you will, without doubt, need to rely on the managers and human resource personnel under your wing. Remember, lead by example. If you don't know the people right under you, then how can you expect them to know the people they are managing?

Too often in business, well-qualified personnel absolutely loaded with talent are right under the owner's or manager's nose and yet you see the company struggle in trying to find a solid candidate from the outside. There may even be a current crisis or a constant problem that the business is experiencing where a current employee knows the solution because of the talent he or she possesses, or has the experience and qualifications to correct the problem with the right solution.

I have even heard of an entrepreneur who, after separating with the president of one of his divisions, went to the three vice presidents and asked them to decide who was going to be the next president of the division. All he wanted was to be informed of their decision by the following Monday! Needless to say, this is not how you run a business. One of the vice presidents did accept the position with the blessings of the other two and failed miserably. It is not surprising that this person and the division did not succeed, since a proper, qualified candidate was not selected. The owner, by his own mismanagement or lack of concern for his business, set up his employees and his business to fail. By the way, those three vice presidents are no longer with this company, a company that is barely alive today.

One of the hiring criteria that you should be cautious of is that of knowing the same people. I have seen the result of an owner who hired a senior sales executive to run the sales department based on the candidate knowing the same people as the owner. The executive mentioned the same people to the owner, shared some of the same general background information he knew about the people, and whammo, he gets the job. This all happened over the course of one business lunch. This person lasted only nine months on the job.

I should also share with you that the owner hired this individual without the consent or knowledge of the person under him whom he selected to run his company. How much of a chance did this situation have to succeed? If you were the president of the company, second in command to the owner, entrepreneur, how much loyalty and confidence did the owner just lose because he went around you, the person he selected to run the day-to-day operation?

The bottom line is this: If you're an owner-entrepreneur and you plan on having someone in charge to run your company on a day-to-day basis, then hire a well-qualified candidate, provide that person with all the tools to do the job, and set him or her up to succeed. Most importantly, help; don't hinder this individual's progress in moving your investment forward.

Chapter 5: Empowerment–Even Caesar Had Generals

Entrepreneur-owners have a very difficult time empowering their employees, specifically their managers, to make decisions in their jobs. Everything from when to go to lunch to what shipping carrier to use, entrepreneurs feel they need to be aware of and in control of every single movement in their business. Don't get me wrong—smart business owners must be involved and aware of where their business stands at all times. However, they also need to develop key leaders in their organization who can make good, sound decisions regarding the daily operations of the business.

Even the great Caesar had generals, so don't think you can do it on your own. Unless, of course, you will be the only person in your organization!

Developing a great management staff—which you may classify as your first set of employees—takes time, it takes energy, it takes resources, and most importantly, it takes an owner who has patience and great interpersonal management skills. If you as an entrepreneur-owner don't feel you have had the training or possess the knowledge to develop a good, solid staff of managers, then take some college courses or seminars. You can check with your local colleges or small business bureau to see what is offered.

The benefit of having a well-trained staff on board as soon as possible is that it will enable you to get some sleep at night. There are enough things that will keep you up at night worrying; you don't need to think about your personnel. Seek and hire great candidates who possess the appropriate skills and knowledge. Look for common sense during the interview process and make the right hire. Hopefully, you will make the right selection and in time, you will have the makings of a great general; one who will help you make decisions, one who can think on his or her feet, one who will allow you more time to devote to the continuing growth and development of your company.

It is always good to remember why you hired your staff to begin with. You hired them to help carry the load, to help you run your organization, to allow you the time you need to be a forward thinker.

If you choose to appoint a manager or group of managers and not allow them the power to make decisions, then don't hire them or promote them. As the owner, you need to be the final decision maker in many situations, however, not in every situation. You must lay the groundwork and the guidelines, so your managers know they have your support when they make decisions. Conversely, they need to know when they have to defer the final say to you. Normally, this will be in the area of expense allocation or a potential change in personnel employment status.

Something to think about; *everyone wants to learn and grow in their lives, both personally and in their careers*. As an owner, if you don't allow your managers and support staff to make decisions, they will never grow to their fullest potential. You must allow them the opportunity to make mistakes and learn from them. Everyone makes mistakes and errors in judgment; if you don't think so, just look in the mirror. The key is to ensure that your staff understands the areas where you want to have the final answer. Apart from those areas, let them manage and guide them through their decisions. Let them know that you are there to help them grow, and that as long as they respect your final decision areas, you will support them.

Remember, the decisions they make—no matter how small or trivial you may think they are—may be enormous in their eyes. So treat each one with a serious mindset and try to make it a positive learning experience for your employee.

If you are looking to grow your business over the long term in sales and profit, grow your customer base and the overall size of your company, then you are going to need a well-trained and qualified group of managers to support and carry this growth. Start now and empower them to make decisions under your guidance; you'll be happy you did.

Chapter 6: Your People, Your Organization

I, like most businesspeople my age, have seen a major shift in the career life expectancy of the average American worker in respect to being part of one organization for your entire career. My dad, probably like yours, retired from the same company he started with. I wish I could make that claim.

My generation has seen many changes in the way companies view their personnel and what is expected from them. Either by their own choice or not, the American worker may very well have more than a dozen different companies listed on his or her resumé by the end of his or her business career. This is true, and as an entrepreneur-owner, it should be of great concern to you for many reasons. *The main reason you should be concerned with this trend is because it has now placed the burden upon you to manage your organization with your employees on top of your priority list, yes, even ahead of your customers!* I can hear the arguments out there already. Let me explain my position.

Your people (employees), when treated well, compensated fairly, and shown a great deal of genuine concern for them and their families by you, will be your greatest asset and ambassadors out in the public eye. They will be extremely loyal to you and the company, work with such enthusiasm and desire to achieve the goals you have set forth that it will be reflected in their overall attitude, especially when it comes to performing their tasks and satisfying your customers. Employees who feel very good about their company and their career opportunities within their company, will by nature treat your customers better and ensure that they will remain your customers over the lifespan of your enterprise.

So, with this in mind, how do you set the foundation for success in this area when you're just starting out? There are two key critical paths you need to follow to achieve success in this area. Let's take a look at them.

The first critical path you must determine is what the right size of your company should be. ***It is better to "right size vs. downsize."*** Starting out, this may be difficult and probably will mean you, the owner, will have to do more of the selling or physical work than you would like to. You may not want to hear this, but I feel this is a good thing for two reasons, especially when just starting out. First, it allows you to control your wage expense in this critical stage of the business. Secondly, it allows you to maintain the feel of the business and stay on the front lines with your employees and customers. There is nothing more motivating for an employee than to see the owner in the trenches with them, moving the business forward. Building a strong team that works well and plays well together will always give you a solid foundation.

I have seen and been involved in many companies where errors have occurred in hiring the right number of people for the current or projected business. I have seen exuberant owners hire people, just to end up terminating them a few weeks later because the business slowed, or something good that they were expecting to occur in the business didn't materialize. One of my most vivid memories of this type of thinking happened years ago, when an owner told me to hire a new staff member because business was going pretty well. After the interviewing and hiring process ran its course and I selected my new employee, the owner came in on the employee's first day on the job and told me to fire her because business was slow. Unfortunately, this type of behavior was an inherent flaw in the owner. He ended up terminating her and I resigned.

My point in sharing this story is this: as an entrepreneur, owner, or manager, your decisions and actions affect more than just yourself; they affect the people around you, your current employees, and the ones you will want to add to your existing team someday. It is better to hire one or two employees fewer and have them busy than to over-hire and have to let them go. As a human being, you should always be concerned that you're doing your very best to treat others fairly. Hiring help without good, sound business reasons, then terminating their services is unacceptable.

The second critical path demands that you *hire the right people for the right job*. This sounds pretty basic and simple, almost to the point of laughable that someone would even have to make this statement. Don't laugh, because there are many companies, especially the small and medium-size ones, that hire very good people but put them in the wrong job. They have a tendency to look at the employee's past job title and not past job responsibilities or capabilities, thus sending that person down the wrong career path within the organization. Owners and managers, including HR departments, need to take more time in evaluating potential employees and current employees to ensure that once on board, they are in the right job and have a clearly-defined career path with the organization. As the owner or manager, it is ultimately your responsibility to ensure that this happens. After all, they are your people and it is your organization.

Chapter 7: Flying High At 30,000 Feet

Entrepreneurs can seriously hurt and even kill the success of their company when they take the ***"suicide management approach"*** to directing their business. This approach to managing your business occurs when you, the owner or manager, feel like everything is going smoothly in your business and that you can now separate yourself from the daily activities. This is a major error in owning a business and you should take every precaution to ensure it is an error you avoid making.

This approach normally results from a feeling of comfort in the owner, where he or she believes that the people down the line have things in control and that the owner's own experience or active involvement is no longer required on a consistent basis. As the primary owner of your business, you should always be actively involved in the daily operation. *This is not to say you should micromanage every detail; however, it does mean you should care enough about your people and the business to ensure that everything is moving towards your current goals.*

I once heard an owner say to a group of people when talking about their employees and their involvement as owners, "we own the company and don't want to deal with the little people." Maybe they should have; their business might still be alive and prospering today. Owners and managers who view their employees as "little people" or people who are below them in status or class should not have the privilege of owning a company. When it gets to a point where you feel you are above your own business and the people who have worked hard to make you and your organization a success, then it is time to consider selling your operation. Why? Always sell when your company is at or near its peak profitability and performance, especially when you are taking the suicide management approach to running the business. The longer and deeper you incorporate this attitude, the quicker the company will decline. Plus, when you have developed such a lack of appreciation and concern for your employees, it will be only a matter of time until the overall performance of your company starts to decline.

Entrepreneurial owners love to fly at 30,000 feet; who doesn't? Their attitude is: *Why can't I? I built this business from ground zero, now I want to sit back and let it just run itself. Or let someone else run it for me.* Take an owner who has run a profitable enterprise and is looking to expand into a related industry. An opportunity to acquire a new business comes along, so he or she jumps on it. The owner does due diligence on the financial end, although not very well, but totally drops the ball when it comes to the personnel he or she will be acquiring. What are their expectations? Are these employees happy in their positions? What concerns do they have coming into my company? How can they help me better understand the business I am looking to purchase? What can they share with me regarding the state of their business and industry? Owners need to get their arms around their most important asset: the people.

The key to this owner's success in purchasing this business is to rely more on the key management personnel of the company that is being acquired, not the owners who are selling it. The key people who are running the day-to-day activities should and will give you a much clearer perspective than the owners who sell it. After all, they want to sell the business!

In the case of the owner who wants to purchase an existing company in a related industry and hire an individual to run it, he or she must be sure to conduct a complete and thorough search for the right person. If you're so keen on keeping your wings flapping at 30,000 feet that you will grab the first person who walks in the door, then don't purchase the company. By not making the right choice in the person who will run this company for you, you potentially condemn the business to failure. You need a well-trained, experienced manager in the specific industry you're buying. They must know how to manage, not just speak or act like they do.

Chapter 8: Train the Trainer

One of the things that the Fortune 500 companies do very well on a consistent basis is "Train the Trainer." What does this mean? Fortune 500 companies do a great job of training their front line managers on how to train and develop their direct reports. Entrepreneurs can take a lesson from these companies by investing in training programs that not only help the manager and employee, but the overall company performance as well.

Well-run organizations place a great amount of value and money in training and developing their employees. The investment of time, money, and company resources is well spent when it comes to the ongoing development of your most valuable company asset, namely your employees. There are many consultants and training companies that can help you develop a well-thought-out custom training program for your employees. After you, the owner or president, thoroughly understand what your goals are concerning your training program requirements, then you need to first set your sights on training your managers. Train the people whom you have selected to train your employees. By not giving your managers specific, detailed interpersonal management skill training, you are laying the foundation for future problems.

Training the Trainer starts with learning how to deal with people—more specifically, with the people you will be managing. Understanding how people think, what people expect in their jobs, what motivates them to perform at the highest possible level, and how to deal with their personnel issues on the job is critical. One of the many things I am most grateful for, after having worked for the Fortune 500 companies I have, is the amount of time and resources they spent on training me to deal with people.

This training has served me well throughout my career and I believe it will for as long as I live.

What separates an average-performing manager from a great manager is the amount of training and understanding the manager possesses when it comes to getting the most performance out of his or her direct reports. Training starts with the managers, then flows downward to the employees. The reason an organization should start its training program with interpersonal management skill development is because it is the most important, yet often the most overlooked aspect of effective management training and development. Although I have seen numerous managers who have been blessed with great inherent people skills, it is not necessary to have been born with them. You can learn and develop these skills. Learning how to effectively deal with the people you are managing should be very important to you, especially if you plan on having a staff that consists of more than just yourself!

Whether Training the Trainer or training the employee, the training initiatives in your organization should never stop. That is not to say that every manager or employee should be in a training session every week, but it should mean that there are established training programs for all managers and employees, and they are scheduled on a normal, consistent basis. Your organization should have developmental programs that are required internally and offer external programs to the employees that are recommended and paid for by the company. These external programs should be made available to help support and enhance the internal training being provided by the company.

Chapter 9: Customer Service–Your Ticket to Future Success

When you hear the words "customer service," what do you think of? What memories or experiences does it stir up? What companies do you think of, both positively and negatively? Customer Service. The words, the terminology, the mission statements, the number one goal of the company, *numero uno?*....Think again.

It still amazes me how many companies tout this as their number one priority, yet fail miserably in its execution. I am just not talking about the entrepreneurial business, but also the big boys. You probably have just thought of several of them right now. Effective customer service can be just as elusive for the national business powers as it can be for the new corner grocery store. Don't believe me? Just go shopping some Saturday and then drive-through a fast food restaurant and you will quickly agree with me.

The problem that companies have in regards to customer service is not in the initiative or goal itself, but in the consistent, day in/day out execution of providing excellent customer service to their customers. It's the blocking and tackling, the X's and O's; it's the basics. We all want to think we have mastered the art of providing great customer service, especially when as a company you have followed a proven training program. ***Unfortunately, companies don't realize that customer service training is constant, nonstop, and requires a great amount of follow-up by management***.

It is the management follow-up and continuing training programs, or lack thereof, that is the biggest detriment to the maintenance of a great customer service program or initiative. Every company talks of having great customer service, but few have follow-up programs that ensure customer service remains a positive attribute of the company they own or serve.

So what do I do to ensure that we are providing great customer service to our customers? Please refer to Chapter 8. If you answered, "train the trainer" you're correct; you nailed this one.

It all goes back to training, not just during a one- or two-week new hire orientation program, but a consistent, everyday training program. Owners and senior managers should be reviewing their customer service initiatives and activity on a weekly, if not daily basis.

Management should be so obsessed with offering great customer service to their customers that they set up independent, outside services to audit and monitor their customer service programs. It is important to note that most companies do have follow-up programs to enforce and evaluate their customer service. However, in many of these cases, it is done internally. When conducting internal audits, the evaluations have a tendency to lean towards the side of the employee. Why? The supervisors doing the evaluation may have a strong bond with the employee and are more sympathetic to their reasons why the minimum acceptable customer service level wasn't met.

You've all heard the message on a call to a company where you have a concern: "Your phone call may be monitored by a customer service supervisor in our efforts to provide you with the best service." Sounds good; maybe these companies in fact utilize recordings of these calls to help in the training of their employees and provide great customer service. I hope they do. It is just too apparent that many companies feel they can just put offering great customer service as a value in their mission statement, and then just walk away from supporting it altogether.

I should mention that in my findings where companies retain the employment of many young adults, there seems to be even more of an urgent need to "get back to the basics of customer services." I do not like to generalize towards a specific demographic group, however, I rewind back to my earlier comment of the Saturday shopping spree and fast food drive-through. I rest my case. Owners of and managers hired to run businesses should trust that their employees are providing great customer service, but also care enough to ensure that it is happening. In all the years of conducting business, all the way back to the first trade between cavemen, providing excellent customer service has been a paramount issue in whether or not you survive as a business.

The companies that understand its importance, live and breathe it daily, and demand excellent customer service from each and every employee are the ones that have found the key to success. *They understand that "meeting a customer need is not enough, great companies exceed the expectations of their customers."* Does your company fall into this category? If not, don't kid yourself; you're losing valuable customers. Customers will continue to support your company now and in the future, provided you show them that you care.

Chapter 10: Customer Service Short Stories–Are Your People in Here?

Here are some short stories with observations from various customer service interactions. You may find these to be humorous; they may seem unbelievable; and they may even wake up some of your own memories. Whatever these do for you, they should at least want you to look into your customer service initiatives and programs. You really don't want any of these to be a representation of you or your company, do you?

The Drive-through

I cannot believe how I can be so programmable. Every time I go to a fast food restaurant and decide to go through the drive-through, I start to remind myself that I will not say "thank you" first, that I will wait to hear those simple, yet sincere words from the local young lad or lady hanging out of the little square window.

After I have thoroughly perused and thoughtfully analyzed my dining options, I place my order. I relay everything I want with great detail, ensuring I allow enough of a pause between entrees' so the order taker can transfer the correct items to the master chef. I hear a garbled, static response back which I think is a confirmation of my order, along with the cost for dinning at such a fine establishment. I am told to pull up to the first window.

My heart starts to race, I remind myself to wait and not say "thank you" first, to see if just once, I will be offered a "thank you." After all, I am the one who is the customer, right? I am the one who—by my patronage of this establishment—is keeping it in business, right? The car slowly rolls up to the window, my arm reaches over, and with my left index finger, I hit the power window button and down comes the window. I am now looking face-to-face with the red-haired, freckled young lad stuck inside the box. The money is exchanged and the goods are delivered into my hands, and now I wait. Nothing! Instinctively, without warning or premeditation, it comes out of my mouth, "Thank you"! Uh, I can't believe it, I had to say it first, but I'm the customer; they should be thanking me! The red-haired young lad with the matching freckles simply looks at me and says, "Yep!" and the window slowly closes. Another chance to win a customer, lost.

Where is the training? Who in the world is running this place? Certainly, this kind of customer service cannot be acceptable to the owners? As I got home and sat at my table preparing to enjoy the dining I so richly deserved, I reached into the sack and "Hey, where's my burger?"

Observation: Customer service is not limited to the adults in our employ; it needs to be strictly enforced even to the youngest of our employees. They need to be taught how to correctly respond to someone who is spending money, supporting your business, a simple but basic common courtesy of saying "thank you" goes along way in keeping the customer coming back.

The Porter

My wife and I were heading for the airport, looking forward to our well-earned vacation away from the world. Taking more than a few days off requires packing more than one bag, and since you pack just the necessities, every bag is important. As we arrived at the airport terminal after parking the car, we had to make the decision whether or not to check our bags inside the terminal or do curbside check-in. Normally, when I travel, I like to check my bags inside the terminal. I don't know why, I just have an unrealistic view that my bags are safer inside the terminal, as if the airline associates inside will somehow take better care of my bags than those outside.

As the lines and people around my terminal entrance became larger and larger, I made the decision that the curbside check-in was the best choice. Proceeding on, we entered the line where our bags would be checked and tagged to our final vacation destination, thus allowing us the freedom and stress release of dragging our bags all over the airport. As we approached the counter, we encounter the "porter." Yes, the "porter," the one guy who can totally throw your vacation plans for a loop faster than you can blink an eye.

After several minutes that seemed more like eternity, we made it up to the counter, showed him our identification and gave him our tickets. During this procedure, the porter did not speak to us or acknowledge us, but kept a very active conversation going with a fellow employee who seemed to have been taking a break at the check-in station we were currently occupying.

When the porter was done processing all the necessary paperwork, he gave us back our airline tickets and baggage claim checks. As we put the tickets back in our carry-on luggage, I noticed the porter staring intently at me as if I had one eye in the middle of my forehead. Several throat clearings and a continuing stare made me a little uncomfortable. I looked back at the porter and noticed him eyeing my bags, bags that were still on the cart, doing this all without moving his head. I asked him if there was anything wrong and he cleared his throat one more time and with a louder than normal or needed voice said, "I'm a porter, sir."

This transaction went on longer than the porter or I would have liked it to go. When things were getting more uncomfortable, a guy behind me said he (the porter) won't budge until you tip him! Upset at this arrogant, self-serving approach to the extortion of a few dollars from my wallet, I waited, then reluctantly tipped him after folding a one-dollar bill so it looked like a million. The robotic servant of the airline industry then started to stare behind me at the next poor soul, the next victim in his 401(K) extortion plan.

As my wife tried to calm me down regarding this blatant disregard for customer service, despite my lack of enthusiastic curbside check-in etiquette, I silently said to myself, "I wonder how my bags will enjoy Paris, I always wanted to go there!"

Observation: if you are in the service industry, remember that your primary job responsibility is to offer great customer service to your customers, regardless of their lack of understanding. There is no room in customer service for "self-promotion"; it is not about how you can benefit from the customer, but how you can serve the customer and keep him coming back!

The Blind Leading The Blinds

My wife and I just moved from a single-family home to a new town home. It took her two years to get me to realize that I would have more time to devote to my interests and reduce my stress if I would give up the lawn mower and put the "for sale" sign in the yard. The sign went up, we sold the house, and "voila"—we're now in the town home and loving it. I now have more time to devote to the things I want to do, instead of all the house and yard maintenance.

The funny thing about buying a new home is that you *really* get a good feel for the state of customer service in our business society today. During this process of new home ownership, we experienced both great customer service and absolutely terrible customer service. Our homebuilder provided the great customer service. They are a very large builder of single-family homes, condominiums, and town homes. The customer service extended to us during and through the entire process was, and still is, nothing short of outstanding. One would think that the stress associated with purchasing a new home would be paramount; however, it was just the opposite. Good for them, they get it!

Stress and frustration always accompanies bad customer service. When customers experience these feelings, you can bet the farm they will never purchase from you again. Companies that don't care about their customers are playing "Russian roulette" with their business. At some point, the chamber that houses the bullet will go off. These companies are totally blind to the reality of the benefits of giving great customer service, which leads me to the terrible customer service story.

After several weeks of painstaking deliberation, my wife—with very little help from yours truly—selected the appropriate style of blinds for our new town home. Most of our window sizes are not standard; they are custom, requiring custom-size blinds. Understand that the amount of time to get the blinds from the company paled in comparison to that of the actual selection process, nonetheless, we persevered. We ordered the blinds from a discount blind broker, if that's the correct terminology, and waited for their arrival. After several days, they showed up on our doorstep. My wife, along with my son who has the patience of the biblical Job, began to hang the custom blinds. (By the way, custom blinds even though they were purchased through a discount blind broker, are still very expensive. On with the story.)

After opening up the various shipping packages, we found out that the brackets needed to hang one of the large custom blinds were not included in the shipping box. Also, another one of the blinds did not contain the wand needed to turn the blinds up and down. After enduring the several weeks of waiting to get the blinds and put them up, I could not fathom the thought of waiting one more day without window coverings. Now I know what a goldfish feels like.

My wife contacted the blind company, explained the situation and they said, "We will get the parts out to you in seven to ten working days." If I'm not mistaken, you could hear my wife's reaction all the way to China! After some negotiation, they reluctantly agreed to ship the parts two-day air. Fast-forward to day three, no parts; day four, no parts; and so on through day seven. Now, understand— during this time, my wife and I disagreed on how and when to contact the blind company, all the time wondering if our 25 years of marriage could withstand the stress of missing brackets and wands.

After the seven-day "grace period," my wife and I gave the blind company, she made the follow-up call inquiring into the missing parts. Not only was she on the phone for over one hour (mostly put on hold by an untrained and somewhat arrogant employee), she also was told that her parts were not shipped. Why? The supplier of the blinds said that the parts were included in the box. Funny, I didn't see one of their employees in my living room trying to install the blinds. Nothing was shipped and nothing was going to get done to satisfy the customer, namely me!

My wife waited on the phone while the customer service representative called the company and requested the needed parts again (or at least I think this was the second attempt). The suppliers argued we received them, but reluctantly agreed to send us the parts. My wife asked the customer service rep if she could talk to an owner, manager, or supervisor to tell them of her dissatisfaction with the whole process. The representative said no, that they talked to a supervisor to get authorization to help a customer, and that was enough. Blood pressure now at 240 over 160! End of conversation.

As of this writing, we have yet to see the missing parts. I hope that by the time I get to the end of this book, I will not feel like a goldfish.

Observation: Never state or imply that your customer is lying about their situation or concern, especially if it is a $1.00 blind bracket. If they're trying to get a $1,000 refund, then take another look at the situation. Bottom line: do whatever it takes to handle problems in an urgent manner. Quick responses with a courteous, helpful, and apologetic attitude will change a dissatisfied customer into a satisfied customer.

The Teflon Manager

I had a conversation with a fellow associate of mine who related a story to me that I would like to share with you. This story should make every owner or company manager sit up and take notice. He related to me that one day he had a meeting in the office of the vice president of sales of a company that he just started to work for. It should be noted here that my fellow associate was the president of another division of this company; by title, he did outrank the Teflon Manager. By responsibility, he didn't.

During the meeting—scheduled to get acquainted and understand how each of them could work together for the betterment of the whole organization—the front-end receptionist interrupted via telephone to explain that a disgruntled customer was on the phone and wanted to talk about the quality of his order. The vice president asked the receptionist if she tried to reach the appropriate salesperson who sold the order to this customer. She said she had tried to reach the salesperson, but could not locate him. The V.P. said to "Keep the guy on hold, and try to find the salesperson again." The receptionist complied with the directive and the two comrades went back to discussing how they would conquer the business world.

About five minutes later, the receptionist buzzed in again to inform the V.P. that she had tried the salesperson's office extension again, left a voice mail, and even tried their cell phone, but all to no avail. The V.P. let out a big sigh, told the poor receptionist—who no doubt was getting more than an earful by now—to go and try to personally locate the salesperson, who must be somewhere in the bowels of the manufacturing facility. (A facility, I might add, that covers more than 200,000 square feet of space, full of little nooks and crannies.) About fifteen minutes later, the receptionist came back to the V.P., this time in person, to inform him that the salesperson could not be located, and that the client was extremely angry that he had been on hold for almost 30 minutes, and that no one, including the V.P. of sales, would address his concerns. The V.P. paused for a moment, thought about it…and told the receptionist to tell the customer that he will have their salesperson call him back. The receptionist left and the Teflon Manager proceeded with his grand plans of world domination.

I do not know what specifically happened after this meeting concerning the follow-up conversations with the upset customer and nonexistent salesperson, but I did find out that the company lost a million-dollar client that day. All because the V.P. didn't care about serving the client, regardless of what the circumstance was or what he would personally have to do to satisfactorily address the customer's concern. The V.P. did not realize what his role was, or understood it and simply didn't care. Either way, for that, he should not be in such a position.

Observation: Regardless of the title of the employee in question, the owner or president of a company must be willing to ensure that all employees "over-service" their clients. When blatant disregard for customer service is being observed, even when the guilty party is a long-time senior manager, companies must react swiftly to address this self-destructive behavior.

On a side note: The V.P. is still running the sales organization!

I am pretty confident that every person who reads these customer service short stories have some of their own that they could share; in fact, I could have included at least a dozen more myself. I have never understood why such an easy concept as offering great customer service has been so hard to grasp by the average business owner or manager. You don't need to have a psychologist give you a lecture on how the human mind works or indulge in some kind of mind-altering drug to find great customer service. All you need to do is sincerely care about the customers, be willing to help them in any way you can, and incorporate this mindset into the daily routine of your employees. It's that simple.

Chapter 11: The Professional Response–I Coulda Been a Millionaire!

Having been on both sides of the desk, I can tell you that the invention of caller I.D. and the automated voice mail system have taken the unprofessional businessperson to an all-time new level. Although these innovations have made our lives easier and much more manageable, they have also crippled the opportunities that are presented to companies each day. *One reason companies miss out on business-building opportunities is because they allow their employees to handle day-to-day business without regard for common professional courtesy*. Although you can see this lack of professional courtesy in many areas of business operations, one of the most abused and misused areas is that of the telephone.

Not only has caller I.D. and voice mail allowed your employees to screen calls, it has taken the personal element of building relationships out of the equation. As owner or manager, ask yourself this question: "How many opportunities has my company missed out on because my employees have not accepted or returned potential business-building phone calls?" If your people were honest with you, you would be absolutely floored to know how they respond, or better phrased, don't respond. In many cases, it goes back to employee training and management expectations.

You may find it elementary or even crazy to suggest that your people take training classes on how to be professional on the phone, return calls and even be, shall I say, nice. As you sit there reading this chapter, don't think that it's only your employees. I've got news for you: it might very well be that you, the owner or manager, are equally guilty of this type of unprofessional behavior. If you are, you are probably unconsciously condoning this behavior. Behavior is learned, so as someone once said, "You must unlearn what you have learned."

This is not to say that every call you receive is an instant million-dollar opportunity; on the contrary, most calls are cold calls from people who are just trying to do their job, make a connection, make something happen. You may not have a need for what is being offered, but it is worth it to get into a practice of listening. Because someday, just someday, it will pay off. It is a very good practice to return every single phone call, explore every opportunity presented, and be professional in every single interaction. In the scheme of things, it takes very little effort to treat others with common courtesy. Remember, those people calling you are also consumers, who have families, friends, and neighbors, who also have families, friends, and neighbors. It goes back to how you are going to be perceived. *Whether or not you plan to accept an appointment with the person who is calling you, or conduct business with them in the future, treat the caller in the same way you would want to be treated.*

Never was this more evident to me than a few years back, when I ran into a person whom I had called on earlier in my career. This person was very hard to get a hold of and enjoyed using caller I.D. and voice mail to screen incoming calls. The only time you could hope to catch him was if he slipped up and accidentally picked up his phone. Which, after several months of trying to contact him, he did. Shocked, he agreed to meet me. A few weeks went by and I finally was able to present my company's capabilities to him. Our scheduled forty-five-minute meeting lasted only ten minutes, because he cut me off and said he wasn't interested in hearing more. I was totally amazed and upset at his unprofessional behavior. The opportunity I was going to present to him ended up going to another company, where they made a ton of money.

Rewind back to my encounter with this person. I asked him how he was doing, and how was the company he worked for. He told me that he left that company after getting an offer to go sell for a different company. He went from buyer to seller! He began to explain to me how he was having difficulty getting a hold of people, having them return his calls, and getting them to agree to make appointments with him. He went on to say that when he could get an appointment there were many times when he wasn't treated very well. I sat back in my chair, took a sip of my drink and had to collect my thoughts before I spoke. I could see he was down. The devil on one of my shoulders gave way to the angel on the other so I went easy on him.

I reminded him of how I went through the same thing with him and that I knew a lot of people who had. I said that although it was difficult, I was able to sell the concept I was going to present to him to another company. I told him that he shouldn't take it personally and that he just needed to keep persevering. He did mention after we got done that he felt bad about how he conducted business in the past, and that now he was getting a taste of what it was like being on the other side of the desk. I often think about this person when I am faced with unprofessional behavior, and wonder why his company never cared enough to help him, train him, and insist that he treat others in a professional manner, regardless of the current state of the business.

It has been several years now, and I am not sure if this person is still working in the same field. Regardless of what he is doing, I do know one thing for sure: He will always treat people with the respect and common courtesy everyone deserves, because he knows first-hand what it is like not to receive it.

If you want to draw a lesson from this chapter, let it be this: Regardless of who it is, why they need you, and what they say they have to offer, respond in a professional manner. Who knows, they may just have a million dollar opportunity for you!

Chapter 12: The Interview from Hell

Being an entrepreneur and your own boss doesn't allow you the freedom to disregard the employment laws set forth by federal and state legislatures. ***More importantly, it doesn't or shouldn't allow you the freedom to treat others disrespectfully.*** Being an entrepreneur doesn't give you the right to be downright mean and cruel.

I was fortunate (or unfortunate, depending on how you look at it) to experience just this kind of behavior in the summer of 2003, when I traveled back East for a job interview. The job had all the things I was looking for in order for me to consider making a job change. It had all the worldly perks, but what interested me most was the opportunity to basically start an organization from the ground level. The parent company had been established for several years and was in excellent financial condition. The company consisted of several partners, all of whom had various management roles in the various businesses they operated. They were looking to hire a person who could take over a relatively young division of their company, thus allowing one of the partners to focus on other business matters.

The executive recruiter who introduced me to this opportunity had placed several people in this organization, and did a very good job of selling me on the company. Prior to traveling back East for the actual interview, I had a phone interview with the senior partner I would be reporting to. The phone interview went well and he certainly liked my resumé. I could tell over the phone that he was an aggressive, take-charge, type A personality. After our phone interview, I informed the recruiter that I would be willing to meet with the senior partner and his business associates. The interview was scheduled two weeks from the date of our phone conversation.

As the scheduled interview quickly approached, I had the opportunity to conduct research on the parent company and found it to be very favorable.

Also during this time, the recruiter had been feeding me information on how the interview would be conducted, whom I would meet, what the partners' personalities were like, etc. I felt very comfortable and secure in my abilities and preparation. I was ready to go.

It should be noted here that I have been blessed to be given the looks that has always made me seem a little older than I truly am. In my early years, let's say pre- and early twenties, it served me well for the things that were important to a young man of that age. Thank God I out grew such behavior. Unfortunately, as I got older, I got heavier and my hair got thinner. Not only thinner, but also gray. Needless to say, for a man of forty-six years of age, it could be said that I look like I could be the next person in line for my AARP card. I kind of like to think of myself as looking, shall I say, "Corporately presidential."

The plan for the day-and-a-half interview was to arrive late Thursday afternoon, have dinner with the senior partner I would be reporting to, then spend all day on Friday interviewing with the other partners and taking tours of their various facilities. Having been brought up in the Fortune 500 business culture and taking numerous human resource classes and seminars on employee relations and practices, I possess a pretty good understanding of proper interviewing techniques and guidelines. I also feel I have a good understanding of how we should treat each other, regardless of the situation or circumstances surrounding the meeting of two individuals.

As I got off the plane and proceeded to pick up my luggage, my cell phone began to ring. It was the recruiter, telling me that the senior partner who was supposed to be there to pick me up was running a little late. A little late, no problem. Forty-five minutes later, my ride showed up.

My interviewer picked me up in a nice new Lexus, and after a quick greeting, began to immediately tell me how old I looked. In fact, I believe his exact words were something like, "I thought I was picking up my grandfather." You can imagine my surprise by this opening comment, especially when you consider that I had to describe my appearance over the phone to him and the recruiter before we actually met.

I did not tell them I looked like a model; I told them exactly who I was and what I looked like. The senior partner went on to tell me that he liked working with younger people, that he liked their enthusiasm, and that he could "out party" them any night of the week. Five minutes into the interview process, I knew I did not want to be their next employee.

We stopped at the hotel so I could check in, freshen up a bit, and then go to dinner. Upon checking in, I found out that the interviewing company had reserved my room, but had not secured it to their credit card. I had to pay for the room myself. It is common practice and courtesy for the interviewing company to pay for all accommodations and travel when conducting interviews. I mentioned this to my interviewer at dinner that night and he did say he would pay for the room the next morning. He did, but I had to remind him twice before checkout.

The Thursday night dinner was a real eye-opener into this entrepreneur-owner. If I thought the conversation in the car about my age was bad, I hadn't heard anything yet. After some general conversation in the car regarding the history of the town I was visiting, we arrived at the restaurant.

Upon entering, I realized that it was a local place frequented by the senior partner on a consistent basis. Although the entire crowd did not say his name out loud when he entered, like "Norm!" on *Cheers,* it was very apparent everyone knew him, especially the ladies. We sat in a corner booth where supposedly we could have some privacy. However, it became apparent he chose the booth so he had a full view of everyone who was in the restaurant and those who would be coming in.

The waitress came over and the booze started flowing—to him, not me. The topic changed from the geographic location and history of the town to my looks. Even as I write this, I am truly amazed at the unprofessional behavior of this businessperson. Anyway, he began to tell me how his partners would think he was crazy because he was interviewing someone as old as I am. Apparently, they too, like to work with young people. Someone who is in his mid-forties must be close to Social Security, right? The night progressed on. I had the opportunity to meet one of the other partners and his wife, who happened to be in the same restaurant. I did say it was a local place.

The partner's wife came over to our booth and planted a very passionate kiss on my interviewer. Understand, at the time of this encounter, I was not aware that this lady was the wife of one of his partners. After a few flirtations between the two, he introduced me as the guy who they're going to interview. A little while later, the other partner came over to join his wife and—I had hoped—to rescue me. He was a nice man, professional, and the only reason I had seen for anyone to join this company.

The night went on and my interviewer asked me very little about myself. He did mention a few resumé items here and there, but we—or should I say he—mainly talked about himself. He talked about how young he looked, how he could get any women in the restaurant if he chose to and (again) how he likes to work and party with the youngsters. After I watched this man drink all night, talk about women and himself, he finally decided it was time to get me back to my hotel, and him back home to his wife. Arriving back in my room well after 1 a.m. east coast time I could not help but feel sorry for this man, and for myself. I thought about calling both the recruiter and him in the morning to let them know that this wasn't a good fit, that I could not see myself in their organization. I literally prayed about what was the right thing to do. The easy thing was to call him on his unprofessional behavior, to let him know how he came across, to let him know that you don't treat people in the manner that he treated me, to let…you get the picture.

The hard thing, but the right thing to do was to continue on with the interviewing process the next day. A full day of anticipating the worst. You may ask why. Why subject oneself to this when you know after the first five minutes of the process you were not going to come on board? The reasons may surprise you.

First, I believe that in everything, in every circumstance, God works things out for our good. *Secondly*, even though I was only a job candidate, I felt I owed the recruiter the professional courtesy to not only finish the interview process, but to put my best foot forward, as the saying goes. *Thirdly*, I believed I wanted to prove to my interviewer and his partners (and maybe myself) that I was the man for the job.

And finally—hold on to your hat—I owed it to the man who the night before had insulted me at least once an hour for six hours. I owed it to him because he did initiate the meeting, paid for my travel, but more important than all of that, he needed to understand that he needs to change his behavior. The only way I could help him see this is to do a great job during the Friday interview process, make them want me, then relate to them through the executive recruiter as to why I would not accept a job offer from them. There they are, four reasons to stay for a full day of Friday fun.

Friday did start out with a few mentions regarding the payment of the hotel bill. After that was corrected, we were off to our first plant tour and to meet some of the people in the company. It was obvious to me that to get to where they wanted to be as a company, some upgrades in personnel would be required within their current ranks, as well as a complete makeover of their current policies and procedures. In fact, the entire business culture needed redirecting. Three hours later, we were off to meet another partner for lunch. This partner was a strategic thinker and the financial guru of the parent company. He was bright and asked great questions. This is where I felt the interview actually started. Since I knew I would not be working for this company, I decided to conduct my part of the interview as if I were an outside consultant. This mindset was helped by the strategic questions that were asked by not only this partner, but also the partner I was going to meet with that afternoon. The same one I met (along with his wife) at the restaurant the night before.

I addressed each question with a well-thought-out, clearly-defined answer. Answers containing strategic thought patterns flowed out of my mouth like Niagara Falls; I completely blew everyone away. (Yes, including my Thursday night dinner partner.) In fact, I was so pumped up—addressing each thought as if I was putting a thousand-piece puzzle together in five minutes—that I only took two bites from my sandwich. And as I recall, it was a very good sandwich. I wished I had the chance to finish it.

From lunch, we went to the next plant tour and to meet the non-interviewing partner from Thursday night. I really did like this partner. He genuinely seemed to be a good person, good businessman; the only thing I couldn't quite figure out is why he would have agreed to partner with the other guy. He certainly had to know what his personality was like. Heck, I knew what he was like within five minutes of meeting the man!

After a few more hours of strategic discussions and giving this partner a blueprint on what they need to do for their newest division, we said our good-byes and I went off to the airport for my westerly trip back home to the "land of normalcy." On the trip to the airport, it was slightly uncomfortable due to the "hard sell" the partner was giving me. I spent a day and an evening with the man and outside of what was on paper, he didn't know anything more about me than he did prior to my arrival. One partner I liked, one partner I thought was okay, and one partner thought I was his grandfather! By the way, this partner, my "would-be grandson," was in his mid-sixties.

True to my word, I did not go to work for this company. They definitely wanted me; I could name my price, all of that. But there is more to life than money, more to life than enduring the stress of working in a situation that you know is not where you need to be. The big question is this: "If the Thursday night senior partner had conducted himself differently, with more professionalism, would I be working for them now?"

Good question. I don't know for sure, but more than likely, the answer would be yes.

The partners forgot one of the major rules when conducting interviews, and that is this: *As much as you are interviewing the candidate, the candidate is also interviewing you.* You are analyzing and determining whether or not the candidate will fit into your organization, your culture, and be able to work with your current team. Guess what—the candidate is doing the same thing.

I know that I could have made an immediate and significant positive impact on their organization. They felt so too, otherwise they would not have offered me the position. It didn't matter; the interview was over after the first five minutes.

Chapter 13: Human Resources–It Evens Sounds Cold & Impersonal

Most companies have taken the "human" element out of the human resource department; for that matter, they have almost taken the *resource* term out too. In well-managed organizations, senior management runs roughshod over their human resource departments. ***There is a very good reason for this, and that is because they expect their HR departments to support, enhance, and cultivate their employees' careers and personal growth.*** They realize that in effort to grow the business, meet the goals established by the owners or management team, and build a solid future for long-term growth, they need a great support team. That support team is the employees.

What occurs in most human resource departments today, especially if they are part of a privately-held firm, is that the HR department has evolved into an administrative, paper-pushing group of people who spend the vast majority of their time making sure the i's are dotted and t's are crossed.

This is not to say that HR departments should not be proficient in administering the various programs that employees are involved in, such as 401(k) and health benefit programs. However, within the current underlying fabric of the human resource department, there is more emphasis placed on administrative skills and processes, versus program initiatives that are aimed at promoting employee career growth. In some instances, companies will even go beyond the career growth initiatives and establish employee programs that enhance the personal, non-business, individual growth of the employee. These programs could be anything from how to manage your household income, personal investing, child rearing classes, how to handle being a single parent, dealing with elderly parents, and spiritual growth programs.

Many human resource departments feel that they need to immediately start out by having numerous programs when senior management decides that what their current HR department is doing is not good enough. The entrepreneur-owner or senior management team decides that they would like to expand or offer more programs for their employees, so naturally, the HR director floods the department with several programs, all of which are good, but overwhelming to the current system and department.

Human resource managers on occasion need to be reminded what their function is in an organization. *Human resource departments should be first and foremost concerned with ensuring that there are well-trained, skilled personnel on staff and available for every functioning department within the organization.* Notice I said well-trained, skilled personnel. Although front line managers have the majority of the training responsibility, as they should, the HR department should be the engine that drives the training car. They need to develop both internal and external training programs to ensure that their number one concern is being met: ensuring that the company has a well-trained, skilled employment staff.

Too often, human resource departments, senior managers, or owners fail to understand the need to cross-train internal staffs. Whether you're a Fortune 500 company with 20,000 employees or you own one store with three employees, cross-training your people to work in other areas of the organization will help you in the future. Not only will it be a great benefit for your organization as you experience personnel changes and shifts in responsibilities, but also it will provide your employees career growth. Growth that they will view as a potential stepping-stone to possible career advancement within your organization. I often wonder why companies don't do more cross-training of their employees. It seems to make a lot of sense to ensure that each one of your employees has developed more than one set of job skills. Expanded knowledge, skill set and flexibility by and with your employees allows an organization the ability to meet changes in customer demand without putting undue stress on the overall organization.

It should be the HR department that establishes a cross-training program for your company. If you're the president or owner of the company, ask your senior HR manager about your company's cross-training program. If you don't have one, I strongly suggest you start one. The only barrier to such a program may be if your company has a union. Unions may restrict movement from one job classification to the other for many reasons. If you do have to work under a union contract, you may wish to make this a contractual discussion point the next time the contract is up. It will only help your business.

I have never liked the term "human resources" or "personnel department." It always seemed so cold, so matter-of-fact, so impersonal. In fact, this department should be the lead department in your organization, as it pertains to career growth, personal growth, and development. *I would much rather see this HR terminology change to something like CPGD department—"career, personal growth & development department."* Now that's a department that feels like it wants to help me succeed in my job and my life! It screams out, "We're here to help you become everything you should and want to become!" Companies that put the good of the company above the development of the employee are missing the boat! When managers put the company first and the employees second, they fail to realize that the employees are the company; this is true regardless if you're a privately-held company or a publicly-traded corporation. Don't believe me? How many companies are out there doing business with no employees?

The major differences between the HR departments of the Fortune 500 companies and that of an entrepreneurial business can be best described as *"culture and expectations."* The business culture developed and grown within a Fortune 500 company dictates that they have a well-rounded, fully-staffed human resource department. The entrepreneurial business, depending on size, may or may not have a staff strictly devoted to personnel issues. Employee expectations should be directed accordingly. If I apply for a job in a Fortune 500 company, or am already working in one, my expectations should be fairly high in what I can expect the company to offer me in the way of both career and personal growth. Conversely, if the company is privately-held, the resources devoted to career and personal growth may very well be limited. In fact, the HR manager may very well be the owner and president of the company. Regardless of the company, the HR department needs to be more than just an assembly plant, spitting out bodies to fill hourly shifts or management positions.

If you are an entrepreneurial owner, you may not have a need for a fully-staffed HR department right now. Your company size may dictate that it is not necessary to have a professionally-trained and educated human resource specialist at the present time in your organization. You may be just starting out or in the early infant years of your company's growth, and due to that, you may be handling the HR area yourself. That's okay and normal for where you and your company are right now.

However, it is important to note that regardless of the size of your company, the human resource element to your company should be well defined and established, ready to meet the needs of your employees, regardless of the number of people under your charge. Just because you only have three people in your company, you still need to allocate the necessary monetary and time resources to ensure you're meeting your employee and company needs in the area of human resources.

Human resource departments should always communicate what developmental programs are available for their employees on a consistent basis. This is to say that it is the responsibility of the HR department to promote both the career and personal development programs the company has to their employees. The promotion or announcement of such programs must occur more than once a year at the annual benefit sign-up meeting. Programs should be discussed with employees on a monthly basis with front line management input. Good HR departments also solicit suggestions from their employees; this could be in the nature of both career advancement need to personal needs that other employees may desire.

Employees need to know that their company's HR departments offer two very important benefits: one, a "quick action" response to both career and personal crisis situations, and two, a "safe haven" for employees, where they can get confidential help and work through any personal issues that may be effecting their work and/or home life.

Companies—regardless of size and monetary resources—that devote the necessary time and energy to help advance both the career growth and personal growth of their employees will reap the benefits by having more productive employees, which means your company will also be more productive. After all, isn't that what you want?

Chapter 14: Retention Plans–Keep the Good Ones!

Companies spend millions of dollars per year on the recruiting, hiring, training, benefits, and salaries of their employees. They think little of spending the money up front to obtain key personnel to fill vacancies in their organizations, yet do nothing to retain the key people who are necessary to maintain and grow the business to new heights. *Companies make a very large mistake when they fall into the trap of becoming comfortable in the mere fact that they secured the employment of a desired individual, relying on the notion that the employee will remain happy, content, and challenged in the company for the rest of his or her career.*

Companies fall into a false sense of security when economic times are tough and unemployment—both nationally and locally—is high. The natural thought process is to believe that the employees, regardless of talent and abilities, will remain with the company because the job market is slow. In fact, many companies take advantage of this situation by applying more pressure on the employees during this time period, or simply taking them for granted. This can be done in a variety of circumstances. It should be mentioned that employees who recognize that their companies are, in fact, taking advantage of them during this period will more than likely start to look for better opportunities when the economy and job market take a positive upward turn.

Taking advantage of a healthy economy and job market demand, or lack thereof, is not limited to companies. During the 1990s, when the economy was flying high, many people took advantage of companies looking to expand and hire more qualified employees. People would even get companies into bidding wars for their services, obtaining five- and six-figure signing bonuses, cars and pre-employment stock options. It was a crazy time, when both companies and employees overreacted to the daily market news. Many employees who took advantage of these years of prosperity were hit in the face when the economy slowed, and we were blindsided by 9/11. Companies that had to get into a bidding war for employee services during these unprecedented years of prosperity have now recoiled themselves to such a degree that they either refuse to offer key employees retention plans or don't know that they should.

It should be noted that not all employees fall into the retention plan category; in fact, probably no more than 10 to 15% of your employees should be under a retention plan. The employees who do fall under a retention program should be those employees—if they left the organization for any reason—whose departure would result in an immediate and negative impact on the business, an impact that would be hard to recover from in the short to midrange term.

These employees are normally your senior staff who have intimate knowledge of the internal workings of your business and those who have strong business relationships with your major client base. Although one would initially think of a high-level person in your organization, a senior staffer, as a person you would want to retain, it may very well be the account manager or administrative assistant who has developed a mutually respectable business relationship with your number one client. ***Remember, the employee you should have under a retention plan is the employee you must have to ensure that your business remains strong and will remain strong in the coming years.***

There are a variety of "retention plans" companies can choose from to ensure that valuable employees stay in your organization. Although there is nothing written that you have to follow a certain predetermined retention plan outline, there are some programs you can implement that will offer you the best chance to retain your most valuable employees.

Probably the most common, yet misused, program is the stock option plan. The stock option plan can be very appealing to key employees of the organization if the stock has a successful track record; or if the company is new, the stock has the potential to pay out handsomely when the company hits its stride. Companies that do have stock option plans need to do a better job of positioning and promoting the stock option plan to their employees and even the executive recruiters the company uses to obtain the services of the employees who would benefit from the stock option. I understand that many companies keep such plans close to their breast so as not to create undue unrest among the general employee body. However, I believe that companies who have these plans would be better off if they were open about them and included employees other than the top executives of the company. Surprised by my inclusion of employees other than the top executives?

If you are, that's good because you should start to look at all of your employees in the same way, regardless of their primary responsibilities. I would make a pretty good guess that there are some very good, very professional administrative assistants out there who carry the weight and workload of some of your top executives. Think out of the box, think beyond the traditional group of employees who normally get the benefits of such programs.

Stock options should be awarded to key employees on a consistent basis. Because stock options are normally tied into the performance of the company, and performances often vary, they are very hard to schedule on a regular cycle, such as awarding stock options on February 1st of each year. In fact, there may be years when the ownership of the company feels that the performance of the company doesn't warrant stock options to be given out for that year. Regardless of whether or not your company will utilize a stock option plan for your employees, companies should be communicating the benefits of employees staying with your company. If you do have a stock option plan, then it should be promoted on a regular basis with clearly-defined entry guidelines for the employee.

I remember the first time I heard about or was involved in a company stock option program. I was a district sales manager for a consumer products Fortune 500 company. Growing up through the ranks, I always heard about how some of the employees paid for new homes or sent their children to college just on their company stock options. Needless to say, I was always hoping to earn this company benefit. It did happen when I reached five years of service and the position of district manager. I was pleasantly surprised by being given 500 shares of company stock. The value of each stock was just under $100 per share. The following week, the stock split and I was well on my way to experiencing one of the greatest benefits an employee could have working for a company: ownership.

Retention programs don't always have to involve company ownership. They can be built into a contractual agreement between the company and the employee. Companies need to balance their thinking as it pertains to hiring and retaining well-qualified, highly productive employees. Companies will expend a lot of time and monetary resources to hire an individual, but will do very little to ensure that the employee stays a vital part of the company.

Including a retention plan in the hiring process right out of the gate is not recommended; however, setting up the potential to do so at a later date is.

As the owner or hiring manager, you would not want to tell a newly-hired employee that he would automatically have a retention plan in his new hire package. However, if you are hiring an employee whom you feel will, in the very immediate future, start to make a significant and positive impact on your business, you may want to include a scheduled time in the future to visit and discuss a possible retention plan.

Let's look at a scenario where you have hired a new senior account development manager. This person's responsibility is to bring in new business to your company and develop new, hopefully long-lasting relationships. You hire this individual, agreeing to a set salary, commission, or bonus plan structure, and the normal company benefits. Although he looks great on paper and has very good recommendations, you still have zero history on how he will perform for your company. Sidebar—if you have never hired an individual who looked good on paper, interviewed well, and had great recommendations, just to find out after a year that they were not going to live up to their or your expectations, then you haven't been in business long enough. That is precisely why you need time to evaluate how the employee will perform before you offer a retention plan.

Let's get back to our scenario on the new business development hire. He has been with your organization for a little over a year and is doing very well, not just meeting your expectations, but actually exceeding them. New business is flowing in, solid relationships are developing between this individual and the new clients, the employee is a very good, upstanding human being, and everything is looking up. You now have a pretty good track record of the value this employee brings to your organization. If you are able to see the value this employee brings to your company, so can your competitors! Now is the time to decide what to do and how to do it to ensure that the employee stays with your company.

Retention programs can include everything from guaranteed bonuses to guaranteed severance plans (a.k.a. golden parachutes) to actual ownership in the company over and above the stock option plan. Regardless of the plans you choose to explore with your key employees, as a smart owner or company president, you should be looking at all options to ensure that your very best people stay with you. Remember, a manager is only as good as the people who work for him. The same is true for the company.

Some organizations include other companywide perks that enhance the desire for employees to stay working for the same company. Although predominantly found in large Fortune 500 companies, these added perks could entice an employee to rethink a position on looking at greener pastures. Some perks include on-site restaurants, hair styling salons, travel agencies, workout and spa facilities, bookstores and reference libraries, day care, car wash, and oil change services. This list may appear over the top if you're not someone who works for a company who offers these to all their employees.

Regardless of your company's financial position to provide these types of perks to your employees, you should, as the owner or company president, do everything possible to offer your employees perks that are above and beyond the normal. ***Don't underestimate the "staying power" these added perks contribute to retaining good employees and keeping consistency within your organization.***

Chapter 15: Corporate Communications–Was There a Meeting Scheduled?

Corporate communications has evolved into a quick response, urgent action method of not only informing your employees about company matters, but also establishing a "real time" lifeline in communicating from companies to their clients. *Communications, both internal and external, within an organization must be geared towards the dissemination of information that will, in essence, provide a quick response to either company issues or client concerns.*

Companies, whether they are a Fortune 500 or an entrepreneurial business, need to ensure that both the internal and external communication initiatives of their company provide the quickest and most responsive means to get information to their designated recipient. We are fortunate to be working in an age when computers and their software systems provide all the necessary tools to communicate our information in a "real time" manner. There is no reason, regardless of company size, that an organization fails to implement the available systems that will aid and support the corporate communication efforts. Due to monetary restraints, small businesses may not be able to purchase or acquire the "state of the art" systems large corporations have. However, if you have a computer and Internet access, you have a corporate communications center.

The e-mail system has allowed corporate communications to be handled in the blink of an eye, or better said, the click of the send button. E-mail systems have provided corporate employees the means to literally run company operations from one site—normally their office or desk location. Inasmuch as this system has helped coordinate, collect, and send out vital information to fellow employees and clients alike, it has also taken out of the equation a considerable amount of the interoffice personal relationships needed to build team cohesiveness and spirit. We all have become "computer geeks" to some degree or another.

The office computer is a must; you need the e-mail system, you need the calendars, you need to be able to develop a spreadsheet, you need to be able to create a sales presentation, and you still need to write letters to your clients.

What you do not need are the games, and depending on what position you have in the company, you probably don't need Internet access either. I know there are many employees who would gasp at this last statement. I would too if I spent the majority of my time at work playing solitaire or Minesweeper, and surfing the Net for my next toy or dream vacation spot. I'm not saying that employees should not have access to blowing off a little steam, or killing some time. However, I am saying that companies would be better served to provide specific locations and times where employees could access these computer-linked items.

One company I worked for did a very smart thing. They designed and built a game room where employees during lunchtime and breaks could go to play video games or foosball, watch television or get on the Internet. The game room was where the employees went to play and the computers located at their desk were where they went to conduct their work.

Every company I have ever worked for has told me during my employee orientation that the office computer, specifically the e-mail system, was to be used for only business e-mails and not for personal e-mails. Let's set this record straight once and for all: **Everyone uses the e-mail system for personal e-mails.** Even if they don't repeatedly sent out e-mails, you sure as heck know that their friends will send some to them. A more realistic approach to this is to allow your employees limited personal e-mail access; however, inappropriate subject matter exchanged between fellow employees and or their friends should be dealt with severely, up to and including termination. Note that all communication vehicles and their proper, acceptable usage must always be explained to the employee during their new hire orientation.

Have you ever heard this line from a fellow associate? "I didn't know we had a meeting scheduled. No one told me!" RRRiiight, you didn't know. You only sent back the meeting confirmation to me via our computer calendar!

We are blessed or cursed—depending on how you look at it—to have the ability to review a fellow associate's schedule for the day, determine a time to set up a meeting, schedule the meeting, and get a response back indicating that the fellow employee will be at the meeting. What did we ever do before this? The problem with this meeting or calendar access is that we have a tendency to abuse it, sometimes rather substantially.

I once worked for an owner who loved the technological aspects of doing business so much in the twenty-first century that all he did all day long was review everyone's schedule and schedule meetings to review his findings with us. We became a company that needed a meeting to schedule a meeting, if that makes any sense. If it does, let me know.

On the subject of meetings—specifically internal meetings—it is always professional courtesy to start and attend meetings on time. So often, I still see this common courtesy being abused within organizations. It's bad enough to have attendees come into a meeting late, but it is even worse when the one who scheduled the meeting in the first place can't even make it on time. The very basics of running a good meeting are to first have all parties arrive on time; secondly, have a predetermined agenda with times designated so everyone understands the meeting schedule and expectations; thirdly, if you are running the meeting as facilitator, keep everyone and the meeting on time; and fourthly, end the meeting on time.

Meeting notes, as well as follow-up action items stemming from the meeting should be recorded and forwarded to all attendees for their implementation. Everyone is on a tight schedule these days and having the ability and understanding to run a very productive and timely meeting will help expedite your daily activities.

Corporate communications consist of every communication vehicle available to and from your organization. Everything from the employee break room garage sale announcement to the employee letter from the owner or president of your company falls under corporate communications. Communications come from all over the organization and because of this fact, it is sometimes hard for organizations to determine who or what department is responsible for them. Some companies assign the human resource department this responsibility, others the IT Department, still others the executive office of the president of the company. In most cases, this is why corporate communications seem to come from all directions and even run perpendicular to each other on the same issues or directives. Companies should develop a "corporate communications center" that will funnel or channel all communication through one department. This department would then have the responsibility to direct, edit, and ensure that all communications are cohesive and are in line with all corporate directives.

The key is to have a designated person or department in charge of all communications, where they have not only the responsibility, but also the accountability to ensure all corporate communications directives are being met.

If you're a small business with three employees, it is still a good practice to have one designated area from which to channel all communications. You don't need to be a Fortune 500 organization with many resources to run a smart, well-organized company that subscribes to and implements great communication practices.

Chapter 16: The Tortoise & the Hare–Place Your Bets!

Strategic planning versus daily activity; situational analysis versus a knee-jerk reaction; the Model T versus a Ferrari; The tortoise versus the hare.

Companies, both large and small, are reactionary, meaning they all react to changes in business. They react to what their competitors are doing, what the stock market or shareholders say about the company's performance or direction. They even react when the local business owner's spouse states that he or she doesn't like the current direction of the business.

While all companies are reactionary, a smaller percentage could be classified as proactive. A proactive company has created, developed, and implemented a prescribed program that enables it to be the "first" in its industry to bring either products or services to the marketplace. Being a proactive company is not limited to the big boys; smaller businesses should be just as capable of being the first to market in their respective business as their big brothers. In fact, a smaller, entrepreneurial company has a huge advantage over a large Fortune 500, in that it can by pass the normal bureaucracy or "red tape" that is inherent in a large organization. That's the good news. The not-so-good news is that a smaller company may not have the financial ability that a larger company has, thus reducing the opportunity to get your product or service to the marketplace in a reasonable timeline.

Overall, large corporations do a very good job of long-term strategic planning. They incorporate their executive staffs, from marketing to sales to operations, and together develop plans that will enable the company to sustain marketable growth over a future specific period, normally three to seven years out. Plans will encompass all areas of the company and will run parallel to the main goals and objectives set down by either the board or major shareholders. Changes in their business environment normally will not shake the large companies, and although they do adapt and react to these changes rather quickly, they remain firm in their commitment to stay on course regarding their strategic initiatives.

In contrast, smaller, entrepreneurial companies in general do not do a very good job of strategic long-term planning, not because they don't go through the process, but more so because they have to utilize more of their available resources to react more quickly to changes in their business environment. The smaller business does not have the luxury of unlimited resources like the Fortune 500, both monetary and in personnel to address these changes without either abandoning or steering way off course of their long-term plans. *This is why it is important that the small business plan not be overly aggressive when starting out; they need to take the tortoise approach, not the hare.*

Whereas the Fortune 500 company has the ability to adjust to these changes without major disruptions in their operations, the small business entrepreneur must aggressively attack the challenge to his business to maintain its position, or simply ensure that the business stays open. Larger organizations have a great advantage in that they can analyze the data causing their business environment change, throw resources at it, review the current situation, and formulate a well-thought-out plan of attack. The small business owner and his team have to be more reactionary to the data, leaving themselves open to a higher margin for error should their solution or countermeasure be proven wrong.

The same rules that one would suggest to a smaller, entrepreneurial company to follow when planning, executing, and adjusting to surprise changes in the marketplace are the same ones you would expect to find in large companies. The rules to ensure a higher rate of success would be to develop a short and long-term plan, build in a safety net, including a reasonable amount of time to adjust for changes that may cause you to have to veer off course, a plan to reset or refocus back on the original plan, and build or secure the necessary resources to support the plan over its lifespan.

The entrepreneur owner, at times, can put his or her own company in trouble because they either did not formulate a long-term strategic plan, are not working the plan they did create, or the plan they did create was flawed. This inability to follow a long-term plan creates the knee-jerk reaction to every situation they face. Decisions are made on the fly, action is taken without analysis, and the risks start to be larger than the rewards.

Although strategic planning is needed throughout the lifespan of the business, it is never more important than in the very beginning, in the formulation of the company. The entrepreneur can make a significant error in judgment in determining up front that the rewards of the enterprise have already exceeded the risks being taken on.

This conclusion all before they have even sold their first product or service. This type of thinking—although kudos should be given for enthusiasm—can set up the small businessperson to become far more extended financially than necessary in the early stages of their business. The desire for immediate success replaces the need to ask themselves a series of questions before they go out and invest in more equipment than is currently needed, hire more people than are currently needed, and veer off of the original business plan they just developed before there is any reason to make such an adjustment.

Small business entrepreneurs, as well as senior managers, need to ask themselves several questions before launching a new business initiative. For example: What are my most immediate investment needs to get started? What are the very basic elements I need to be able to open the doors? What items can I put off or delay purchasing or investing in until my business volume warrants the additional investment from me? Do my anticipated startup costs, in both equipment and personnel, reflect my original short-term and long-term business plan? Am I willing to extend my time and energy to ensure I grow the business in a systematic and profitable manner?

The last question really is the one that will determine your direction. As mentioned in a previous chapter, the entrepreneur-owner, or senior manager directing the business initiative, needs to be willing to sacrifice his or her own personal time, energy, and even monetary resources to ensure that the new business enterprise does not take on more risk than what the company can afford.

It is important if you are an entrepreneurial owner just starting out, or in the infancy of your company, that you start out slowly. Develop and work a very specific strategic plan; build in a safety net to be able to adapt to unexpected changes in your business environment; thoroughly analyze every situation; then proceed with a well-thought-out action plan that will reduce your risk and ensure that you have the best possible chance for success.

Remember, everyone would much rather drive a Ferrari than a Model T. After all, the Ferrari will get you there much faster, but will also elevate the risk that you may not get to your destination safely. Though the Model T is considerably slower and less exotic, you can be assured that you will get to your destination safely, and who knows, you may just be able to enjoy the scenery too!

Chapter 17: Building a Working Environment to Guarantee Success!

Building a working environment for success in your business is not about making sure that you have all the "bells and whistles" on your business computer, it is about your people.

Developing an atmosphere within your organization that promotes team unity, a sense of belonging and acceptance, appreciation and fairness, and fulfillment, both in terms of business and personal growth, is the primary responsibility of the owner or senior manager of the organization. Too often, it is the little things an owner or manager can do for one of their employees that are overlooked. The owner or manager feels that the employee cares only about the money, the title, and the benefits. The responsibility to provide an honest and fair wage and benefit plan falls directly on the owner or management board that runs the organization. It is right to provide these to every one of your employees. If you are doing this now, great— you're doing what you are supposed to be doing, what you signed up to provide when you started the business in the first place. You don't get a "pat on the back" for doing just what is expected and right for your employees.

Companies that subscribe to the management policy of just paying their employees a wage and throwing in some benefits are missing out on the best part about running an organization, or more importantly, owning an organization. That is, demonstrating that you, the owner, sincerely care about your employees, not just as workers, but also as human beings, people with feelings, people who have concerns, people who are just as intricately wired as you are. Most people in their jobs want to work for owners who see above and beyond the mindset that the company is paying you a salary. They want to work for an organization that does the little, unexpected things for their employees, both on a group and individual level. Whatever your company decides to do above and beyond the normal, it should be done with sincerity. ***Don't be fooled by making an assumption that your employees will accept any insincere act as true sincerity.*** People are much smarter than you think, including your own employees.

Creating an atmosphere for success starts well before doing the little things for your employees; it starts with the owner or manager demonstrating to the employees that they possess the right attitude about work, the right attitude toward their employees, and the right attitude towards business in general.

Showing your employees that you care about them and appreciate their contribution to the company's success is not a "once in a while" proposition. It must become a consistent habit, a consistent behavioral trait you demonstrate daily. ***"Don't just say it, live it."***

I have heard the same thing on numerous occasions from totally different people, in different time zones and at different times in my life: "It would be nice if the boss just recognized my efforts, what I do for the company; it would be nice to just be appreciated." When your employees are making these types of comments, you are not only failing as a boss, you're failing as a human being. It has taken me years to figure out this question: "What is worse, being unable to recognize what your employees need, or knowing what they need and not being willing to fulfill them?" If you said the latter, I'm in your camp. It is far worse to know what someone needs, have the means to do something about it, yet refuse to act on it, knowing full well that it will be a benefit or blessing to that individual. The trick is to find out if the owner recognizes the need.

There are many different ways an employer can show his or her employees that the company cares about them and recognizes their efforts towards accomplishing the goals of the organization. Remember, *it is the seemingly insignificant things or expressions of gratitude that will endear an employee to his or her company and/or owner.* Many times, these expressions contribute to the employee's happiness far more than the monetary rewards. If you don't believe me, ask an outside consulting firm to conduct a random audit. Although not 100%, the majority of the employees would rather work for a company that appreciates them, has a personal interest in them and their families, and treats them as if they were their own, than just give them a raise and never think twice about the person inside the worker.

Simple things, like handing an employee who has been going above and beyond his normal job responsibilities sporting event tickets for him and his son would go a long way to say "we appreciate you."

Think about the amount of time that the employee has sacrificed away from his or her child to get the job done right and on time. How about the same scenario, but a dinner for two for the employee and his or her spouse? Maybe it's an extra day off with pay; how about a round of golf, or a spa gift certificate for the employee who has been under the stress of meeting a long and ever-changing client deadline? It can be as easy as a surprise lunch for a long-time loyal employee. Sometimes, just sometimes, it is as simple as stopping by an employee workstation, extending a hand and saying "Thank you for all of your hard work. I really appreciate it and it doesn't go unnoticed."

Employee recognition programs are a vital link to the contribution of building a successful working environment. Many companies, however, do not place enough emphasis on these programs. They call up the employee—or e-mail them—and say, "Congratulations on your five years with us, now feel free to pick out your bread maker or toaster." Recognition programs should be personal, well-thought-out, and significant enough to endear not only the employee to the company, but also other employees who see how the company truly values their contribution and loyalty.

Group activities, such as company picnics, holiday parties, birthday celebrations, potlucks, and the like, all seem to help build team unity. The key to these company events is to make them different and fun. There is nothing worse than having to attend a boring company event. You want your employees to look forward to the event and by their own excitement create an atmosphere of togetherness and unity that will permeate the entire organization. Having occasional "get-togethers" will not be a substitute for the daily need to be involved in the personal and business lives of your employees. Companies that understand this are already one step ahead of their competitors.

Chapter 18: Everyone Is a Salesperson

I once heard an owner of company say that everyone in his organization was a salesperson. He was right. Whatever your employee's official title is in your company, whatever his or her primary responsibility is in your company, he or she is first and foremost, a salesperson. As I mentioned in a previous chapter, your employees are your best ambassadors to help you promote your company in the public eye. Whether your employees are administrative assistants, buyers, technical support staff, production workers, creative designers, shipping clerks, whatever they are, they are still all salespeople first. Remember, your employees do come in contact with people who either work with your company, or know of people who may purchase or use a product or service your company has to offer.

So what about the actual designated salespeople in your organization? If everyone is a salesperson, what does that make them? It makes them one of your most valuable assets since they have been designated as the front line client contact to develop and grow your business. This is why I have always had a problem understanding why, when business is soft, companies immediate look at reducing the sales force in their organizations. That is not to say that a company should not address unproductive salespeople; in fact, evaluation of employee performance should be ongoing, whether they are designated salespeople or not. What I never could understand is that the sales department— whose sole responsibility is to bring in sales—always seems to be the first area to reduce head count when it matters the most. Simply said, when sales are slow, the knee-jerk reaction is to eliminate positions in the sales department, instead of evaluating the current performance of the sales staff and upgrading its personnel. ***Companies should increase their sales effort when sales are slow, not compound the problem by reducing the number of company contacts calling on your clients.***

Salespeople are a unique animal. They love the face-to-face contact with clients, they thrive on the hunt for the next order, they love competition, they need the gratification that comes with placing a new order on the boss' desk, and they like the compensation.

This is why companies treat their salespeople a little differently when it comes to flexibility of schedule, expense accounts, and compensation plans. Everything else should always be equal to that of every other employee. Companies should allow certain guidelines to be different for salespeople, and salespeople should not abuse these special considerations given to them by the company.

It is important to note that there are really three kinds of salespeople: Order Takers, Maintainers, and Hunters. **Order Takers** are those individuals who do not possess the skills to research and develop new business contacts, they possess average interpersonal management skills, have difficulty handling rejection, and enjoy receiving positive results on a consistent basis.

Maintainers are those salespeople who have limited ability and knowledge of how to research and develop new business contacts. They do possess good interpersonal management and social skills, but do not have to or want to worry about penetrating deeper into the client structure. They enjoy maintaining the status quo.

Hunters are those individuals who thrive on researching, targeting, and bagging the next big client. They possess very strong, almost aggressive skills in finding and developing new business. They have outstanding interpersonal management skills, can demonstrate the ability to penetrate all levels of a client's organization, handle rejection well, and have a relentless attitude and strong desire to succeed.

A company that has a need for a strong sales organization will need to develop, cultivate, and blend a group of Order Takers, Maintainers, and Hunters if it is to succeed and maximize the sales potential of the organization. The simple truth is that there is little crossover between these three sales groups. For example, you would absolutely eliminate the Hunter's ability to do his or her job well if you were to ask that person to become either an Order Taker or a Maintainer. Why? The Hunter would immediately feel underused, limited, unchallenged, and quite frankly, be bored out of his or her mind. Conversely, if you asked an Order Taker to become a Hunter, he or she would feel enormously pressured, overmatched, underdeveloped, and fearful.

The Maintainers are the ones who have the most flexibility to either go up to the next level or down. The reason for this is that they possess a representation of both the Order Taker and Hunter characteristics.

Although many people are born with certain personal characteristics predetermined at birth, most salespeople can be trained to develop the skills necessary to elevate them to a higher position where they can tackle and achieve a greater level of both personal and business success. Understand that there is absolutely nothing wrong with being an Order Taker or a Maintainer for a company, just as there is nothing special about being a Hunter. It is important for you, the owner or manager, to fully understand this. Your business has or probably will develop to the point where you will see the need to have a mixture of all three of these sales individuals in your organization.

Each salesperson's ability and desire to succeed should be based upon his or her own performance and what he or she contributes to the overall success of the company. As owner or manager, it is ultimately your responsibility to accurately define what sales role your employee will play. You can determine this in a variety of ways, including but not limited to specific personality testing. Many times, it can be as simple as asking your potential salesperson what he or she likes and doesn't like.

If they like something or show interest in a specific area, or it shows up as strength in a test result, then develop them through a sales development-training program. Who knows, you may just have found your next great Hunter.

Chapter 19: So What Does Your Company Do?

I have heard this question many times over during my career, and regardless of what my company did or didn't do, I always answered it honestly. I know that may sound somewhat strange coming from a person who has spent most of his life in the sales management arena. After all, aren't most salespeople known to spin a yarn or two in their sales pitches? Nope, not a good idea.

Marketing yourself or your company as someone or something you're not usually results in a catastrophe. You might as well hit yourself on the head with a hammer or shoot yourself in the foot. This chapter is not about "how to" market your product or service, it is about the mindset of properly marketing your company. Although I could go into detail on marketing your product or service, there are plenty of good books on the subject.

Entrepreneurial companies, especially new upstarts, have a real problem in this area. The excitement and freshness of starting their new endeavor very often overshadows the calmness that is needed to properly position their company in the marketplace. *The desire and willingness to be everything to everybody, not miss a sales opportunity, and get their company name out in the public ends up creating an immediate identity crisis, one which many businesses are not prepared to deal with.*

Presentations where you say you have the capabilities or knowledge to handle a project and don't, open up the black abyss where many companies wander aimlessly, trying to find their way back into the light. The sales or capabilities presentations where owners, managers, and salespeople suggest that their company can do certain things and can't, fail to acknowledge that your customers are smarter than you give them credit for. Although they may give you the order, or assign you the project based upon what you have told them, it will only be a matter of time before your "stretch of the truth" is exposed, usually accompanying some sort of monetary loss to your company.

I worked for a few entrepreneurial companies where the owners had a saying, a saying that they believed and lived by. It originated and always followed a meeting with a customer who asked them if their company could handle a certain aspect of a job.

Their saying to the customer was, "Yes, we can do that." Then after they left the customer, they would say to themselves or their employees, "How are we going to do it?" In one respect, they deserve credit for having such a great, entrepreneurial spirit—possessing the "can do" attitude. However, putting yourself and your company in such a position causes a domino effect in your organization that you may not be able to recover from. Let's take a look at an example.

An owner secures an appointment with a client to discuss and present his or her company's capabilities. The presentation material works well enough to spark some interest on the client's part, so the client, based upon what was presented, asks some further questions about the capabilities of the company. The owner replies that yes, they have the capability to perform such duties in fulfillment of the client's desired goals. The two parties agree to work together and the project is birthed. The owner fully understands that they neither have the capability in house, nor know where to find someone who does. The client assumes and has taken the entrepreneur on good faith, that in fact, they do possess the capabilities necessary to fulfill the requirements of the job. Already, the road to success has been split in two. Both roads will result in two unwelcome outcomes.

The owner now must make some quick and probably some unresearched decisions to hold onto the new business that was just secured. If the project or order commitment requires a product to be produced and you don't have the machinery to do it, do you go out and buy a machine that can do the job? If you get the machine, who will run it with proficiency? What's the cost of the machine and will you be able to use it at a later date? Was this machinery and its capabilities in your business plan? And if it wasn't, but it is now, what changes do you make to your long-term strategic business plans to include this new capability? How does the pressure of feeding this new beast affect how you go to market? What financial burdens have you just incurred that may prohibit your company from either staying in business in the future or maximizing its potential? Does this sound like strategic marketing positioning?

If the nonexistent capability is a service, which requires the addition of a new person to your staff, it may not be as financially risky as a new capital expense, but it is still a risk nonetheless. The same series of questions I just posed can be directly related to the addition of a staff person who was not in the original strategic marketing plans of the company. In fact, this one would have a more significantly negative impact because you are dealing with a person, a person who has value and worth. Mismanaging a person, hiring someone who doesn't fit into the current marketing plans of your company just because you committed something you shouldn't have to a client, is inexcusable.

The project moves forward, in both decision-making to fill the need, and time. The owner continues to give "warm fuzzes" to the client, letting them know that all job aspects are being handled and on time, all the while there is utter chaos back in the owner's company. Time and money are being wasted in an attempt to present an acceptable, high-quality component to the client.

Days go by, then weeks, and an acceptable solution has still not been realized. The client starts to get worried and concern that what was agreed to will not be met. They face the unthinkable, telling their boss that the order will not be fulfilled on time. The dominoes start to fall. Realizing that the owner will not be able to adequately fulfill the order request on time, the job is pulled and given to another company. Although already late, the client feels that they are better served by taking their business elsewhere, taking the "better late than never" attitude. The client's job security has now been compromised within their own organization because of the project delay and undue pressure it caused within the various relying departments.

The owner and his or her company now sit, left with the remnants of the error in judgment presented weeks ago. The resources, both in terms of finances and personnel that have been expended over the short lifespan of this one project, are monumental in their losses. Your company's marketing position, strategic plans, and financial structure all lay in ruins, fragile at best.

To top all of this off, your other clients are starting to turn up the heat on you because you have spent so much time, energy, and resources on this one project that their projects are falling way behind. The projects that your company is more than capable of performing, for those clients who will potentially keep coming back to you and that you can build a solid business foundation on, that fit into your strategic marketing position, the "good projects" and client relationships you now have just put in jeopardy.

Positioning your company in the marketplace should be strategic, meaning it should be well thought out and clearly defined. Who are we? Who aren't we? What are our capabilities? What do we do well? Which opportunities will fit our strategic position? Which ones won't? Are we willing to turn away business that does not match what we offer as a company? Who or what clients or customers are our target audience? How do we stay on course and ensure we don't fall off?

If you haven't asked yourself these and other similar questions when determining your company's marketing positioning before the doors opened up, then you are already walking a thin line between success and failure.

If you have, but you haven't reviewed these questions and your answers to them in a while, you may want to start asking them again. Especially before your next client meeting; you just might save yourself and company some grief.

Chapter 20: Wait Before You Hit That Trap Door...Handling the Non-Performing Employee

I would like to know how many lawsuits are filed each year by employees who seek fairness and compensation from entrepreneur owners whom they feel have terminated them without justification. I know that many states have a "right to work" law, which basically allows an employer to terminate the services of an employee for any reason. The only problem I have with this wording is that it should read, "justifiable reason." Entrepreneurs walk a tightrope with no safety net when it comes to disciplinary action taken against an employee. Regardless of the legal implications of such action, both in favor of or against an owner, there is a process that supercedes the outright termination of an employee. ***That process is communication, evaluation, determination, and re-assimilation, what I call the CEDR process.***

Before an entrepreneurial owner or one of his managers terminates a non-performing employee, it is well worth their time and energy to implement the CEDR process. Not only does this process allow you, the owner, to effectively address the performance issue of your employee, it also allows you to do it in a fair and honest manner. Employees who have performance issues almost always come back to the beginning: "I was never told what was expected of me." Before you can utilize the CEDR process, you must have an employee who has been given the right to know, understand, accept and perform the job duties for which he or she was hired. ***You cannot morally or ethically address employee non-performance when the employee has no idea what he or she is being corrected or reprimanded for.***

Assuming your non-performing employee has been told what is expected of him, what his job duties are, and he has been given regularly scheduled reviews by his immediate supervisors, then and only then do you have the "green light" to use the CEDR process. When an employee's non- performance or wrong behavior comes to your attention, you should do a couple of things before implementing the CEDR process.

First, you should thoroughly discuss the findings with the supervisor who is reporting the problem, to ensure you have all the accurate information. In doing so, you want to make sure that the problems that are being presented are factual, not hearsay. Secondly, you should review all past personnel reviews and records to see if there have been previous problems, if you are not already aware of them. If everything you have been presented is factual and you deem it necessary to take corrective action, then start the process.

First, *Communicate* with the employee. Schedule a time where you will not be interrupted and make sure that the employee's immediate supervisor is in attendance, if it is not you. If your employee is a female, I strongly suggest that you have a female supervisor on hand even if she is not her direct report. The reason for this is so that there will not be any room for or accusation of impropriety when there are two genders alone discussing corrective measures. Discuss the issues or concerns that have been presented to you regarding the employee's performance.

Talk openly and honestly with the employee. Outline how his or her performance is not up to the standards of the company and reiterate what is expected of him or her, and how and what he or she is being measured against. Listen to the response; you may uncover some other problems you were not aware of. Establish the corrective measures and a timeline by which you expect the performance to be enhanced and brought up to acceptable standards. Write these down on a formal review format and have all parties sign so everyone is in agreement. Set up a future date to review the employee's progress. This should be within 30 days of your initial meeting.

During the time directly after the meeting, you and your supervisor should be ***Evaluating*** the performance of the employee to see if he is working towards improving his performance, and to see if the effort is being made to meet the minimum standards for employment. This time should also be used to have casual conversations with the employee and show him your support in his efforts to turn his performance around. You should not isolate him, or isolate yourself from him during this time. Observations on his work performance during this time should be written down for the next evaluation period.

After the designated period of time is up, you should conduct the follow-up meeting with the employee and the appropriate supervisor.

During this second meeting with all parties present, a ***Determination*** should be made on how the company and the employee will proceed going forward. At this time, if you the owner and your supervisor feel that additional time is needed to evaluate the employee's performance, then a new meeting date should be scheduled for two to three weeks later. Note: This process is not meant to keep the employee on edge or looking over his shoulder for the remainder of his employment life with you. Be fair and don't abuse the process; that could cause emotional harm to the employee. If it is determined that the employee has made the necessary changes, corrected what he needed to correct, then formalize the meeting and the results achieved. During this meeting time, reinforce the performance or behavior that the company expects from the employee and re-establish a new regular review date. Make sure all parties sign the formal review.

Once the communication, evaluation, and determination steps have been completed, then it is time to **Re-Assimilate** the employee back to the work force. This sounds more technical than it is. Re-assimilation is just allowing the employee to feel like he is once again back in the family fold, held in high esteem, and valued for what he contributes to the organization. This final step does not eliminate the problem from ever having existed. All documentation from this entire corrective action should be kept in the employee's personnel file, not to be thrown back at the employee when an owner feels like "juicing up" the troops. It should be kept in the file for reference should the problems surface again, or as a compliment to the employee who showed that he could in fact turn his performance around and continue to make a significant contribution to the company.

Unfortunately, there are times when corrective action, even repeated corrective action, done in a fair and honest manner, falls short and the employee needs to be terminated. Under this situation, you now have the written documentation to present to anyone who would challenge your decision. This documentation will show that you dealt with the employee in a fair and impartial manner, that you gave the employee every opportunity to correct his behavior and demonstrate the minimum acceptable standards required for continued employment, and that the employee, by his own decision, did not desire to implement the corrective action needed to maintain his job. Not only is this a personnel management method that works for the company, it is also the right thing to do for your employees.

A few more comments regarding your decision to terminate an employee: It should keep you up a night or two, regardless if you know it is the right decision. Employees are people, people who have pride, dignity, and self-worth. It is your responsibility as the owner or manager to separate from the employee in a professional, caring manner, even if the employee is upset. Every consideration should be given to providing adequate severance pay to the terminated employee. Many companies, after terminating employees, give no severance pay to the employee. They must, by law, pay the employee any unused vacation pay earned and for the work done through his or her last day of employment; however, severance pay is another issue.

Some companies will give two weeks' pay, or a week or two for each full year of service. Organizations that don't fairly compensate the employee for losing his or her job need to evaluate their policy, or better said, institute a new, more "real world" policy. Research, find out how long it would take for the average employee—given his or her current abilities—to land a new position with another company. Be fair and do right by the employee. *Analyze your part or company's part in the situation that caused the termination. You might be surprised to find out that due to some deficiency in your management policy, process, or structure, the failure of the employee can be linked back to something you or your company failed to do.*

The cost of paying severance to terminated employees should be factored into your annual budget because it is inevitable that as an owner you will be faced with this situation. If you go a full year without even having to think about it, consider yourself fortunate. The monetary cost of providing severance to terminated employees should be, in itself, enough motivation to have you and your management teams do everything possible to train and motivate your employees to work above the minimal acceptable standards. If you face challenges in this area—and you will—then just implement the CEDR process and get them back in the family. You'll be glad you did!

Chapter 21: Silos Belong on a Farm

Webster's Dictionary defines a silo as a large, airtight tower or pit. Interesting, I have lived in some, not the ones usually found on a farm, the ones found in companies all across the country. Predominantly found in the entrepreneurial business, they can also be found in large corporations as well.

What is a business silo? It is a department, a division, or even a separate stand-alone company that externally presents itself as an integral part of another business unit, yet internally contains no processes or direction that supports such external claims. These business silos are created in part by the accountants in a company solely based upon the fact that they like the new or acquired business unit to show they are worthy or profitable enough to be a significant contributor to the overall parent company. It is understandable and right that each business unit or function of a company must be able to stand on its own and be a profitable contributor to the company. However, when you allow the financial balance sheet to dictate how you go to market, or how the company departments work and flow together for the good of your overall organization, it is time to make some changes in how you are managing your company.

Large Fortune 500 companies have more difficulty making such changes in their organizations for several reasons; one is that most corporations these days are being run by financial people, where 10 to 15 years ago, most CEOs came from a sales and marketing background. Financial people tend to think in terms of black and white, or better said, dollars and cents. They have difficulty looking past the accounting methods and looking for the best possible structure to support long-term profitable growth, even if it means a short-term financial loss in the process.

Entrepreneurial companies have a great advantage in this area because they do not have the large corporate "red tape" layers normally associated with companies of size.

This is why it is difficult to understand why an owner of an entrepreneurial company would allow the way he or she structures the company to be predicated on what a single department contributes financially to an organization.

Let me give you an example.

An owner of a company buys a business unit of another company that parallels that of his current business. The newly-acquired business fits very well with the current business and many departments within the newly-acquired business unit are almost an exact duplicate of current existing departments. The owner of the company decides to keep the new business unit as a separate stand-alone business, although both businesses are under the same roof. After several weeks, the newly-acquired business unit is not losing money, but is not as profitable as the owner would like.

The owner, understanding that there are certain departments that could be combined, decides to continue to keep the newly-acquired business unit as a separate business, even though there would be great synergy and cost savings associated with combining departments. The unwillingness, stubbornness, or just sheer lack of attentiveness by the owner is causing undue stress, duplicated efforts, miscommunications, and a financial drain on both material and human resources within the company. This lack of change results in putting the measurement of how well the newly-acquired business is doing on its own over the good of the company. The thought process by the owner is that he would not have purchased the company if the long-term prognosis of the new business was not good. Therefore, why would the owner not structure his organization so it would be the most efficient and profitable one he could possibly have?

Owners and even the CEOs of many corporations, at times, feel like they cannot change the structure of their organizations to complement internal departments, and better position themselves in the marketplace. They are reluctant to change because of the time and the financial implications of making such moves. Many times, though, it boils down to what I had previously mentioned, which is the lack of attentiveness or stubbornness. The latter being the attitude of, "I'm going to make this work my way, no matter what it costs."

It is important to remember what business silos are in terms of your organization. ***Business silos are organizational and structural roadblocks that can be bypassed; they are barriers that can be knocked down, leaving the path open to establishing a well-thought-out, clearly-defined organizational structure that will put your company on a solid course of profitable growth.***

If you are buying a company outright and not merging it into your existing business, then obviously it must be profitable and be able to sustain long-term growth. However, if you buy a company that contains the same or similar departments to those currently existing in your company, then manage the merger so your company can maximize its potential, both in profit and growth.

Chapter 22: Circle the Wagons!

One of the most important and best things you can do for yourself and your business is to surround yourself with people who are honest and reliable and have integrity. I am not just talking about your employees, I'm talking about your business associates and contacts.

If you currently have a business or are planning to open a business, you need to secure several relationships that are necessary to help you start your business, or be active in the overall managing of the business. You need to ensure that you have a great attorney, one who knows everything about starting a business and one who knows what will probably be needed in the way of legal counsel over the lifespan of your business. The attorney you select should not only know business law, he or she should practice it on a daily basis. I would recommend that the attorney, or his or her law firm, devote at least a third to half of its billable time to general or governmental business. Why do I recommend this? It is pretty simple. ***Whatever the reasons are as to why you need an attorney, for business, establishing a will, divorce, bankruptcy, you want someone who has daily experience in the area you need.*** It's common sense, so pay particular attention to the attorney's and the firm's general makeup and expertise. If possible, I would look for a smaller to medium-size firm— these are firms with anywhere from fifteen to thirty-five attorneys. The reason for this is that it will allow you to develop a closer business relationship with your attorney, it will be easier to have access to your attorney with regards to fitting you into his or her schedule, and more important, the relationship will feel more "down home" and personal. There is also nothing wrong with the big law firms that exist everywhere, especially in the downtown metropolitan areas; I just prefer a smaller firm with great expertise in the area I need.

Another relationship that you need is with a great certified public accountant (CPA), who not only knows the federal and state tax laws, especially when it comes to business, but who literally studies and keeps abreast of the ever-changing tax laws that are passed throughout the year. It is important to remember that when you are in business, you will need your CPA on a much more frequent basis. At the very minimum, you will need to sit down and have a formal meeting with him or her once per quarter.

It is even more helpful if your CPA is also a certified financial planner, one who not only can help you with your taxes, but also help you in your personal, as well as your business investment planning. Like the attorney and his or her firm, I would suggest a small CPA firm or an independent CPA who has an impeccable reputation and is accessible to meet your needs.

Whether you are just starting out, have been in business for a short while, or have been in business for years, you need a good bank and a strong personal relationship with the primary bank loan officer. Depending on where your business is in terms of its size, growth, income, and profitability, choosing the type of bank to deal with should be relatively easy, provided you keep your ego in check. If you are just starting out, find yourself a small bank, one where you can develop good relations with the loan officer. ***You want the loan officer to know all about you, what type of business you're entering into, and what your goals and expectations are.*** Also, it makes sense that if the potential business loan you're looking at obtaining is relatively small—say under $100,000—you have a better chance getting a loan from a smaller bank that specializes in small business loans. Some larger banks that deal with large corporations may prefer to work with only their large clients, ones that are borrowing in excess of one million dollars on a consistent basis.

Another business contact you will need to secure is a good insurance agent. Preferably, you will want to look at finding an independent agent, one who can shop multiple companies and find the best coverage and rates you will need for your business. Coverage such as major medical and health, long-term disability, liability, property, life, and malpractice insurance may all be required, and *it is best to have someone who can find you the best possible coverage at the lowest possible price.*

When starting out, you will no doubt either talk with your CPA or attorney first. When you ask them your specific questions pertaining to their expertise, *don't forget to solicit a recommendation for your other business contacts.* Your CPA probably already works with a very good attorney and vice versa. The same holds true with your banker and insurance agent. Ask each one for a few referrals and then interview them to see if you want them on your team. After all, it's your business; you will be paying them for their services, so you should feel comfortable with them.

Once you have your business support team in place, you can rest assured that you will have more than adequate help, protection, expertise, and counsel to help you run your business and reach its fullest potential.

Chapter 23: It's a Family Affair

If you're starting a business, or currently own and operate a business, more than likely you have at least one family member working for you. In fact, you may have many family members in your employ—your spouse, son, daughter, brother, sister, niece, nephew, your third cousin on your spouse's side. You get the picture. If this last description is your business, that's perfectly all right. If you have no further aspirations than to provide an income for as many family members as you can, there is certainly nothing wrong with that.

For those of you who see your entrepreneur business growing well beyond the "nuclear family business," there are some managerial pitfalls you will want to avoid. Those pitfalls will lead to employee dissatisfaction, envy, and loss of productivity or worse. There is nothing wrong with having family members in your organization, provided you set strict guidelines and policies on what is acceptable behavior—behavior that is acceptable in the business environment and behavior that is not. Internal family matters, personal issues shared with only family members should be kept completely out of the workplace. Discussions regarding these personal issues should be restricted to outside the exterior office building. I realize this seems rather harsh. However, it is only fair and right for your other non-family employees that no family member be treated with special consideration in front of other employees.

I know that expecting your immediate family member to be held under the same policy and guidelines as other employees may be very difficult for you to handle. However, if you set the parameters right from the beginning and outline your expectations, you will be able to integrate family employees and non-family employees together. *In contrast, if you don't do this well or choose not to do this at all, then you will never experience the growth potential your company may currently possess.*

A company that employs family members within its organization has a unique managerial situation that does not exist in companies that choose not to allow nepotism within their doors. Many organizations still will not allow family members to work in the same company or at the same location for the reasons I mentioned above. As an entrepreneurial owner, you have a choice to make. Will you allow family members to work for you and your company, and if so, how will you establish company guidelines and policies to ensure that everyone can work well together and be productive?

I have seen and experienced entrepreneurial companies that have been successful in this area, and some that haven't. The ones that have been, treat all family members like their other employees and those non-family employees know it. In addition, those family members respect and honor the guidelines established to ensure everyone is treated equally. *They do not abuse the "bloodlines" that exist within the corporation, in fact, they go out of their way to make sure that they are invisible.* These organizations tend to look and feel more like a Fortune 500 in terms of environment because the company is managed without special acknowledgment or obvious considerations to family members.

The companies that have had difficulty in this area are those where set, written policies and guidelines have not been established. They operate by the "seat of their pants" and bring family issues into the workplace. The owner of the business allows and even falls into the same trap as the family member who fails to realize that the dirty laundry needs to be cleaned outside the business, at home. They fail to realize that the expectations of the family member in question should be equal to that of other employees.

So what do you do if you're experiencing this problem now in your established family business? First, make sure you institute new policies regarding how you will handle future problems. Secondly, share these new guidelines with all family members and in general, with all employees. Thirdly, address the current situation with the employee family member in question and get the problem handled, but make sure you do it after hours, unless it is specifically work related. And fourthly, make sure going forward you treat them like you would every other employee. Doing this will make for a less stressful family reunion the next time one rolls around.

Chapter 24: Self-analysis–Changing Your Management Behavior

In the beginning of this book, I mentioned that the book would challenge how you think, act, and conduct your business as an entrepreneurial owner. Also, that you will need to check your ego at the door, and that if you were not willing to do so, you should drop this book and run fast, very fast. Thanks for not running and for allowing me the privilege of sharing my experiences, observations, and thoughts with you.

Now that you have read this book, how do you go about making a change in your management behavior? How do you correct and redirect your thought processes, actions, and expectations so you can achieve the long-term growth potential that you seek for your company?

The first thing to do is conduct a "self-analysis." This is going to be hard and you may not like what you find. The good news is that you will be happy that you addressed these issues, because it will then allow you to make changes in how you manage that will not only benefit you, but your company and your employees.

Start out by examining your current and past behavior and actions. Think back to situations where you had to make a managerial decision regarding your business. This could be how you handled a personnel issue, how you went about developing your initial business plan, how you handled the purchasing of another company, how you conducted an important interview, or how you handled a serious customer service problem.

Solicit opinions from your family members regarding how you handle similar matters or issues away from the workplace. The answers you hear may confirm a behavior pattern that shows up at work and in the way you handle your employees, customers, suppliers, and fellow business associates.

Select a few of your most reliable and loyal employees, the ones who have been with you for a long time, the ones whom you not only value their service, but their opinion as well.

Now, if you cannot immediately think of a few employees who fit this bill, then your journey may be harder than you think. ***Regardless of whether you have employees you feel you can go to and solicit their opinion, you should hire an outside independent source to create and conduct an impartial, anonymous survey covering your employees' feelings and opinions on what they think about the company and the owner or managers of the company***. In doing so, you will be presented with a very clear view of what your biggest ambassadors (your employees) think of you, your management behavior, and their overall feelings of working for you and your company.

If you want to reach your goal of positively changing your behavior, then you will need to be open and honest with your employees. Tell them why you're asking their opinions, tell them you want to be a better owner and manager of their company. Tell them that you want them to be proud of where they work, the customers that they serve, and their future as a significant member of the company family.

When you receive the comments and opinions back from your employee survey, you will be faced with a very important decision. How do you handle the criticism and negative comments concerning you, your management style, and their impression of the company that provides a job for them? Do you immediately build a defensive wall between you and your employees? Do you arbitrarily lash out at employees because you're angry at their responses? Do you look to blame others for specific comments? Remember why you asked for their opinion in the first place. You, the owner or senior manager, wanted to effect a positive change in how you managed the business and its number one asset, the employees. So then, what is the correct response to this information?

The correct response to this information is to evaluate it with an open mind. Look for patterns and for opportunities where you can effect immediate positive change, and where the areas are that you will need to develop plans to effect long-term positive changes. Share the results of the survey with your entire company. Again be open, honest, and willing to announce and implement at least one positive change during your initial meeting. If several comments reflect negatively on the way you run the company, evaluate them honestly. If they're right, make a concerted effort to change your behavior so your employees can experience first-hand your desire to make work a better place. *Remember, great leaders lead by example. If you want your employees and company performance to change, then you have to be willing to change first.* Otherwise, lock the door and throw away the key.

After your initial post-survey meeting, you will want to select a small group of employees to help you effect the desired change your organization needs.

Set up action plans to determine the plans that are needed to make the correct, positive changes you and your team desire. Outline a step-by-step process with targeted implementation dates to ensure all items you wish to change are addressed and completed in a timely manner. Items should be prioritized in order of importance, but pay close attention to those items that can be done quickly. ***This will demonstrate to your employees that positive changes are being made quickly, and this alone will improve morale and productivity, and allow you the time needed to make corrective changes on the larger issues.***

It is important to note here that if the change needed is one where you, the owner, need to make a change in your management behavior, including how you treat and handle your employees, then make the change immediately. Do not delay. Seek whatever assistance you need to make the change. Remember, if *you* won't change, you cannot ask others to or expect them to follow you as you try to direct a change in your company.

As you progress through the step-by-step process of change, make sure you build into your plan those steps where you stop and audit your progress to date, making sure the action items you've already implemented are being done on a daily basis and are now part of your standard operating procedure. Constant evaluations should be done on a regular basis, including a formal monthly employee meeting where you, the owner or senior manager, discuss the company's progress. Your progress should be tracked and the efforts of each initiative should be published and shared with your entire company. ***Celebrate your achievements, use these victories as continuous steps to improve your team spirit and unity***. Use these to further rally your troops to complete each and every change you have set out to accomplish.

When every item has been addressed and changed, turned into either a company policy or a new behavior, then you should evaluate your progress on a yearly basis. A new employee survey should be sent out to see how well you achieved your desired goals, test the new temperament of your employees, and see if any new issues have developed. If you make this an annual program, then over time, you will find that your employees are not only meeting the goals of your company, but also exceeding them on a regular basis.

Remember, it really does all start with you, the owner and manager. You set the tempo, you set the direction, you set the rules, you are the only one who can set your company and people up to succeed. It is a great responsibility and a privilege. Do not take it lightly.

Services Available

CS Business Consultants & Marketing Solutions, Inc., based in Minneapolis, Minnesota, offers consulting services in the areas of:

- New business sales development practices
- Sales management organization & development
- In-Store merchandising program evaluation & management structure
- New product marketing solutions

Contact Information:

Paul Balus
CEO and President
CS Business Consultants & Marketing Solutions, Inc.
15722 France Way
Apple Valley, MN 55124
651-269-3048
p_balus@hotmail.com